James Horsley

Lays of Jesmond and Tyneside

Songs and Poems

James Horsley

Lays of Jesmond and Tyneside
Songs and Poems

ISBN/EAN: 9783744775434

Printed in Europe, USA, Canada, Australia, Japan

Cover: Foto ©Thomas Meinert / pixelio.de

More available books at **www.hansebooks.com**

LAYS OF JESMOND

AND

TYNESIDE SONGS AND POEMS.

BY THE LATE

JAMES HORSLEY.

———

Newcastle-on-Tyne :
ANDREW REID, SONS & CO., 50, GREY STREET.
ALLAN, BOOKSELLER, BLACKETT STREET.
———
1891.

TO

LORD AND LADY ARMSTRONG,

WHO HAVE,

BY THEIR MUNIFICENT GIFTS,

LAID THE

INHABITANTS OF TYNESIDE UNDER A DEEP DEBT OF

GRATITUDE,

THIS VOLUME IS, BY PERMISSION,

RESPECTFULLY DEDICATED.

Sir William! to your genius and your name,
The praise of men can add but little fame,
But stout Northumbrian hearts would not be true
If silence was their only gift to you.

To Lady Armstrong and to you we owe
More than mere words of gratitude can show;
Munificence like yours, so great, so rare,
Enduring marble should alone declare.

And yet, what marble or what fluent pen
Could mark your place among our greatest men?
Your works of genius, enterprise, and skill,
Themselves are monuments that nations fill.

Born in our midst, it is our boast and pride
To claim you for ourselves and dear Tyneside;
And though no native honours may you crown,
Your name reflects on us its great renown.

How shall we all your deeds of kindness praise?
For each new gift fresh thoughtfulness displays;
Man's noblest form of life you seem to live—
You live to labour and you love to give.

The church, the hospital, the school, our health,
Have each to own your fostering care and wealth;
But over all, our hearts most touched have been
By this—your gift of lovely Jesmond Dene.

Accept, Sir William, the unbounded thanks
Of every resident on Tyneside's banks;
May Elswick, Cragside, Jesmond, all proclaim
Your worth, your enterprise, and world-wide fame.

PREFACE.

THE publication of this volume is largely due to the desire, repeatedly expressed by many of Mr. Horsley's friends, that his poetical pieces should be collected and issued in book form. With the exception of a four-page *brochure*, entitled " Lays of Jesmond," which he published in 1880, and again in 1884 on the occasion of the Prince of Wales' visit to Newcastle, Mr. Horsley, for various reasons, did not see his way clear to comply with these requests. Since his death, however, it has been thought advisable to do so, and they are now issued in the hope that they will commend themselves to the admirers of Tyneside Poetry and Song.

Several of his miscellaneous pieces appeared from time to time in the *North of England Advertiser*, the *Daily Chronicle, Daily Journal*, and *Newcastle Courant*, and also in other daily and weekly newspapers of the district when the circumstances which gave them birth were the current topics of the day.

No particular order has been observed in their arrangement, with the exception that those referring to Jesmond (Mr. Horsley's favourite theme) have been placed first, then the miscellaneous pieces, and lastly, those in the Tyneside dialect.

It will be noticed that in several of the songs in the local dialect, the mode of spelling the same word differs somewhat. With few exceptions there has been no alteration made in the style adopted by Mr. Horsley; and it has been thought advisable to print them as they were originally written.

Thanks are due and are hereby tendered to Messrs. R. Ward & Sons, Newcastle, for permission to insert the Prize Songs which appeared in the *North of England Almanacs* from 1880 to 1888; to the Editor of the *Weekly Chronicle* for the Prize Poem, " Kindness Everywhere ;" to the proprietors of *The Cyclist* for the Song entitled "The Bicycle Bell," which appeared in the Christmas Number of that publication for 1882; to Messrs. Thomas and George Allan, for copies of several broadside songs which were issued by them ; and to all others who have assisted in their publication.

SKETCH OF THE LIFE OF
JAMES HORSLEY.

James Horsley (the writer of these Poems and Songs) was the son of James Horsley, farmer, Snipe House, near Alnwick, by his second wife. He was born in 1828, about which time his father removed to Newcastle, and attempted a small business in Percy Street. The venture did not succeed, owing to what cause is not known. In a few years both his father and mother died. He was thus left an orphan at an early age, with little education, with no means, and without a friend. Such are the facts contained in the few lines of auto-biography that the author has left on record. How he managed to struggle through those trying years of early life, without home or friends, is, to a large extent, uncertain and problematical.

At one time he was a cabin boy in a coasting vessel, or collier, sailing between the Tyne and London. He has related that one of the crew, with whom he slept, was an inveterate smoker, and would go to bed with his pipe in his mouth, and even when asleep would be drawing away at it long after it had gone out.

At another time he was errand lad with a grocer in Newcastle, and used to practice French on the top of the sugar casks with a piece of chalk.

His precarious mode of living caused him frequently to remove from one situation to another. He would seldom hesitate to give up a job if he thought he saw a chance of bettering himself in an entirely new occupation.

He was for some time employed by Dr. Shiell, of Regent Terrace, Newcastle, as message boy and general servant. It was, no doubt, while thus employed in Dr. Shiell's house and surgery that he acquired what little knowledge of drugs and medicine he possessed, and upon which in after years he often acted when any trifling ailment attacked him.

When about eighteen or twenty years of age, he found a good deal of employment about stables and horses. It was when so employed, he once had a very narrow escape from being killed by a powerful stallion. Going into the stall to feed the animal, it suddenly reared up, and would have crushed him, had he not, with great presence of mind, seized it by the neck, and, being a small active lad, curled himself up out of the way of its forelegs, while it endeavoured to get him under its feet. He held on bravely till an opportune moment arrived, when he let go his hold and slipped out of its reach.

Living about the stables, he was frequently called up during the night to attend to gentlemen's horses which arrived late. He often started very early in the morning, going with a gentleman as far as Morpeth, when he had to ride the horse home again bare-backed. He would sometimes fall asleep on the animal's back from sheer exhaustion, the horse picking its way home as well as it could, without his guidance.

After a few years of great vicissitudes (and how great these vicissitudes may have been we can scarcely conceive), he became connected with *Ward's Directory*. This would be about the year 1850. The printing office was in St. Nicholas' Churchyard, the first door on the right after ascending the steps from Dean Street. Mr. Ward afterwards removed to the foot of Dean Street next to the railway arch, where he fitted up hot and cold water baths, which Mr. Horsley for some time took charge of. He was afterwards employed as canvasser and collector for the *North of England Advertiser*. About this time his health gave way, and he was laid up for a considerable period.

In the beginning of 1859, he entered the service of Mr. Andrew Reid (who was then in business in Pilgrim Street) as collector and canvasser for the *Railway Guide*. In 1860 he had another long and severe illness, which confined him to his bed for some months, during which time he devoted himself to the earnest study of the Holy Scriptures. His frequent conversations with his most intimate friends, and the readiness with which he could quote passages from the Bible, were evidences of a mind well stored with religious truth. Doctor Lightfoot was his medical attendant at this time, and, during one of his visits, Mr. Horsley asked him if it was at all likely, in the event of his recovery, that he would be subject to a recurrence of the attack from which he was suffering. Doctor Lightfoot replied that it was quite likely he would be. This knowledge did not distress him. He was always of a lively and cheerful disposition, and for thirty years after this he continued to discharge his duties with credit to himself and satisfaction to his employer.

He was a great favourite with his associates at Printing Court Buildings. In the social gatherings and annual outings in connection with the establishment, although not always able to be present with them, his presence was always welcome and eagerly looked for.

His anxiety for young men coming from the country to Newcastle, was very marked. Those who had the pleasure of his acquaintance and the privilege of his friendship, can bear testimony to the sound advice given them. "Be careful of the company you keep," he would say, "and be thoroughly honest and truthful in all your dealings." Not a few it is hoped have profited by his counsel and example. He was of temperate and abstemious habits, yet neither parsimonious nor niggardly. His maxim was—"Live within your means, no matter what your salary may be, and never get into debt." Upon this plan he acted himself; and knowing as he did that he was not a robust man, but might be laid aside from his daily occupation at any moment (as he sometimes was), he was careful to make what provision he could against " a rainy day."

He was a great admirer of nature, and delighted to wander amid the sylvan beauties of Jesmond, every foot of which was to him as enchanted ground. His " Ash Tree," "Spring's Evening Hour," "Jesmond Dene," "The Grove," &c., all evidence the love he had for this charming locality. No Saturday afternoon excursions into the country could tempt him from his favourite spot. He preferred to revel in the profusion of vernal grandeur nearer home.

The duties of his occupation caused him to be a frequent visitor to the English Lakes. To these visits he attributed the awakening of the poetical faculty within him. The varied scenery of that delightful locality was undoubtedly favourable to the cultivation of the muse; but no spot in his estimation excelled Jesmond Dene and its surroundings for variety and beauty.

For twelve months or more before his last illness, he was far from well, and seemed gradually to be getting more and more unable for the discharge of his duties. About the middle of November, 1890, he was advised to confine himself to the house, and take complete rest. This he did; but from that illness he never recovered. He soon began to be missed from his accustomed rounds in business circles, and frequent enquiries were made about him in the most kindly terms, and many expressions of sympathy were tendered to him during that time. For the comforts he enjoyed and the attentions he received he was ever grateful, and spoke in the highest terms of the kind consideration he had always received from his employer.

A few weeks before his death, it became evident that he would not recover. Conversation with friends who called began to be a trouble to him, owing to his extreme weakness, and few were admitted to see him. The writer of this short sketch visited him up to the day of his death, and can bear testimony to the uncomplaining spirit he manifested during his affliction, to the firm faith he exhibited in Christ as his Saviour, and to his deep gratitude to God for all his goodness to him and care over him during his whole lifetime. He was careful not to give unnecessary trouble to those who waited on him, and his gratitude and thankfulness were manifested up to the very last. The love he bore to those who were dear to him is strikingly manifested in the beautiful lines of his given on page 47.

On Sunday, the 8th of March, 1891, at the age of 62 years, he quietly breathed his last, and gently passed away, respected by all who knew him, and lamented by a large circle of sorrowing friends.

IN MEMORIAM.

J ust drop a tear upon the tomb of him who's gone to rest ;
A las, no more the vital spark will move that quiet breast.
M anly and upright was his walk while travelling here below,
E vincing naught of selfishness nor yet of outward show.
S weetly and softly on mine ear in gentle accents fell
H is tribute offerings to the muse—the muse he loved so well.
O ft in his wanderings forth at eve did his poetic mind
R ejoice in nature's loveliness and true enjoyment find.
S erenely now methinks he stands amidst the white-robed throng,
L istening with eager ears to learn the angels' ceaseless song.
E ternity's bright morning dawns ! ye angels louder sing !
Y e everlasting doors ope wide, and let the traveller in.

W. II. HASTINGS.

The following obituary notices of his death appeared
in the local papers:—

From the " Newcastle Daily Journal," March 11, 1891.

A well-known form and face amongst the tradesmen of
Newcastle and district will be seen no more owing to the
death of Mr. James Horsley, which took place at noon
on Sunday. Mr. Horsley was for upwards of thirty years
in the employment of Mr. Andrew Reid of Printing Court
Buildings, as manager and editor of *Reid's Railway Guide*,
and no one outside the offices of the North Eastern
Railway was more conversant with the ramifications of
the railway system of trains than he was. He made the
"Guide" his study from month to month and year to
year, and had travelled over nearly all its branches in
the four adjacent counties, both in winter and summer,
and knew every branch in connection with the main
lines. The deceased gentleman was a native of Alnwick,
but when quite young his parents removed to Newcastle,
and both died when Mr. Horsley was very young in years.
Previous to his engagement with Mr. Reid, he did valu-
able service for the late Mr. Robert Ward, when that
gentleman first published his *Directory of Newcastle* and
the adjacent towns; and also in connection with the
North of England Advertiser. He was also an occasional
contributor to its columns, and was fond of literary
work; on more than one occasion he wrote the Retiort
Keelmin's Lokil Letter when there was likely to be a
disappointment in its issue. He was fond of poetry, and
his verses have often found a place in the *Journal* and
Courant. A few of his finest pieces, entitled "Lays of
Jesmond," he had printed some time ago. His songs in

the local dialect were very happy, racy, and to the point;
notably those on "That Blessed Corporation;" the one
written during the time of the great snowstorm eleven
years ago; and his "Twenty-fower o'clock, Man," when
all the stir was made about the change in making the
clocks with twenty-four hours instead of twelve.   He
was of a gentle and kindly disposition, and his sympa-
thetic ear was ever ready to listen to the cry of distress.
He has left behind him a host of sorrowing friends, and
his fellow-labourers at Printing Court Buildings will miss
his cheery word and kindly greeting, and no one more
so than his esteemed employer, whose confidence and
esteem he retained to the very last.   He was a faithful
servant and a true friend.   He was a conservative in
politics, and an exemplary churchman.

From the " Newcastle Weekly Chronicle," March 14, 1891.

Mr. James Horsley, a gentleman well known in Newcastle, died on Sunday at his residence, 42, Chester
Street, Newcastle, at the age of 62 years.   His parents
belonged to the ducal town of Alnwick, but his father
removed to Newcastle when James was quite young,
and, both father and mother dying shortly afterwards,
he was left at a very early age to make his way in the
world as best he could.   He was never of a strong
or robust nature, but was able to discharge his
duties until the end of last year.   Ever since the week
before Christmas he had been confined to the house,
and died on Sunday morning last, at the age of 62 years.
The deceased was best known amongst the tradesmen

in Newcastle and surrounding districts through his long and honourable connexion with Mr. Andrew Reid, for whom he edited the *Railway Guide*—the "Bradshaw of the North." For thirty-two years he was Mr. Reid's valued and trusted servant, and enjoyed that gentleman's trust and confidence up till the very last. Mr. Horsley was of a literary turn of mind, and was an occasional contributor to the columns of the local press. Previous to his engagement with Mr. Reid he assisted the late Mr. Robert Ward in the compilation of the well-known Newcastle Directory. He also wrote verses which have appeared in the columns of the *Daily* and *Weekly Chronicle*. He was a strong advocate for the claims of the Dicky Bird Society, and gained one of the first prizes given by Uncle Toby for the best song to commemorate the enrolment of the 100,000 names in that society. His "Lays of Jesmond"—a little *brochure* which he printed some years ago—contains some of his finest pieces on the beauties of Jesmond. He also wrote several songs in the Newcastle dialect, two of his best being "Newcassell and the Snaw-storm" and "Twenty-fower o'clock, Man." The funeral took place at St. Andrew's Cemetery, on Wednesday, March 11th.

"Robin Goodfellow" in the "Weekly Chronicle,"
March 14, 1891.

The death of Mr. James Horsley, which occurred at his residence in Newcastle last Sunday, removes from among us one of those patient, plodding, and unobtrusive sons of toil and song by whose quiet labours the community in which they move is made happier, and life itself more enjoyable. Mr. Horsley was an observant wanderer in the by-paths of local history—a contributor for many years to the local press of curious and out-of-the-way bits of information relating to departed worthies, decaying industries, and half-forgotten manners and customs of past generations. His admiration for Tyneside was unbounded; his knowledge of its people, and their character and habits, was wide and thorough; and he had a happy knack of preserving in vernacular rhyme the memory of local events which, in the ever-growing pressure of fresh news, quickly fades away. Among these productions of his pen I remember " The Craw's Nest," " Newcassel and the Snawstorm," " Twenty-fower o'Clock," " Corporation Thunder," " Newcassel Dort," " D'ye Knaa John Storey ? " and " Geordie's Jubilee Ode." Occasionally his muse took higher flights, as in " A Pilgrimage " and " Lays of Jesmond "—poetic effusions which contain passages of much beauty and merit.

LAYS OF JESMOND

AND

TYNESIDE SONGS AND POEMS.

A PILGRIMAGE TO JESMOND.

Come with me, friend, together we'll explore
An Oasis at Novocastria's door,
Within whose charmed recesses we shall find
Food and enjoyment for the eye and mind ;
For on our northern coast exposed and bleak
The beautiful is sometimes far to seek.
. Had Grainger realized his early dream,
Fair Elswick might to day have been my theme ;
But Vulcan saw and chose its quiet shores,
Now thousand-handed labour's tumult roars.
'Tis not to sunny Elswick then we'll climb,
Whose brow commands a scene almost sublime—
The valleys of the Derwent and the Team,
The wooded banks of Tyne's wealth-laden stream,
Upon the bosom of whose flowing tide
The argosies of giant commerce glide ;
Nor yet to Arthur's Hill, whose western height
Still more extends the view that fills the sight,
And near to where, a mark of Roman thrall,
May yet be seen the line of Hadrian's Wall ;
Whose buried fragments of a martial yore
Our " Bruce " has made to yield their hidden lore.
'Tis not Imperial Rome we now survey,
We live beneath a less exalted sway—
A sway of passions, and of sordid aims,
Of loud professions and of sounding names ;
Of levellings of denes and ancient towers,
Of bricks and mortar, versus fields and flowers.

A

Still nature lives and smiles in spite of art,
And finds response in every hopeful heart ;
And though encroached upon by human needs,
Spreads where she can her carpet of green meads ;
Such as our noble Moor, whose breezy breast
Invites our footsteps, giving life new zest ;
Where health awaits us, where the eye at will
Can glance from Gosforth o'er to Sheriff Hill ;
Where all alike are free on Freemen's land
To taste sweet liberty at Freedom's hand.
Time was, when homely rural Sandyford
Could those who love rusticity reward ;
Luxuriant hedgerows flanking fields of corn,
With here and there a nook of nature born.
When Lambert's Leap, the Burn, and Cradle Well
For youthful playmates had a potent spell ;
When Friday Fields and Jesmond Gardens led
Young lovers' feet their hedged-in paths to tread ;
When nature unrestrained profusely throve,
And found expression fit in dene and grove ;
Where even yet, in loveliness displayed,
Dwell all her charms in one Elysian glade.

Sweet Jesmond Dene ! 'tis thy umbrageous glen,
With all its dear surroundings, prompts my pen ;
Thy ruin'd chapel, with its holy wells,
That of a "dim past era" mutely tells ;
Thy babbling brook that sings its liquid song
In eddying cascades as it flows along ;
Thy floral banks, thy ravine and thy mill,
Which seem designed the artist's eye to fill ;
Thy paths, thy bridges, ay, thy every tree,
All claim my homage, for they're part of thee ;
And last, though not the least, thy graceful towers,
Whose battlements preside o'er all thy bowers.

I would the gift were mine in words to sing
The beauty born of thee in early spring !
Still more in summer would I long for power
To chant the birth of every opening flower ;

How blooming hawthorn with laburnum vies
In offering incense to the grateful skies ;
How rhododendrons with their " purpling " hue
Seem jealous of the heavens' translucent blue ;
How autumn's foliage in russet brown
Makes autumn's sun blush red as he goes down ;
How limpid ripples on thy purling stream
Smile shining dimples in the moon's pale beam ;
How rich profusion every sense rewards
Made still more rapturous by songs of birds !
Much more thou hast that man hath kindly given
Which makes thee seem a paradise from heaven.
Some fair demesnes where nature captive dwells,
" At home " confined, yet even there excels,
With parks and pleasure grounds—a floral wealth,
Where youth disports itself in joyful health,
Where festival is held with romp and glee,
And dance and game and tuneful minstrelsy ;
Where, transiently released, the sons of toil
Enjoy sweet union with their parent soil.
But here we part, as part must every friend,
Our pilgrimage indeed may well here end ;
For after contemplating hill and dale
'Twere meet to part in Jesmond's lovely vale.

Pons Ælii ! thou treasured Roman gem !
And relique of the Norman's diadem ;
Thy heirs have won for thee a worthy name,
And for themselves a never dying fame.
In classic art, in learning, science, skill,
They each a lengthening scroll of history fill ;
And nature, too, thy stream hath so endowed
With gifts, of which thy sons may well be proud !
And Jesmond's of them whose poetic sound
Doth sweetly harmonize with sylvan ground.
Then ye who love the beautiful and true,
Read nature as she here appeals to you ;
And as ye draw out from her wells of truth,
Renew your purity, your health, your youth ;
And with each draught in thankfulness and love,
Lift up your thoughts to nature's God above.

JESMOND.

O, Jesmond ! Jesmond ! much I love thee,
Thy memories round my heart entwine ;
Thy landscape ever seems more lovely,
Thou fair suburban gem of Tyne.

In youth I've revelled in thy sweetness,
And fondly watched, when little known,
Thy budding forth—thy rustic meetness
For all, to which thou now art grown.

Should I desire the morning's brightness,
The lark's clear carol in the sky,
The early dew, the airy lightness,
All these thou richly dost supply.

Or, should I long in sorrow's chillness
To muse among the silent dead,
Thy Cemetery's mural stillness
Shall tempt my soft and pensive tread.

Or, should I seek communion nearer,
With hope and trust two hearts between,
With her, whose love to me grows dearer,
I'll wander in thy sylvan dene.

I've travelled far, I've travelled widely,
And some of earth's fair scenes have known,
But far or wide, there's none beside thee,
Hath charms that soothe me like thy own.

Thy walks, thy grove, thy murmuring streamlet,
Thy homes of wealth, thy meadows fair ;
These all fulfil my happiest dreams, yet—
Not one, not one, my heart can spare.

JESMOND DENE.

Thou fair lovely dene, with thy rippling burn,
Surpassing in beauty at every turn,
Thy forest of verdure in serrièd ranks,
Thy meandering walks and thy flowery banks.
Say, where shall Elysian glades be found
To rival thy valley, oh Jesumound ?
Oh for a Wordsworth ! Oh for a Scott !
To give thee a voice, thou beautiful spot.

THE CHAPEL RUIN AT JESMOND.*

Once hallowed pile ! no longer to thy fold
The pilgrim comes his evensong to hold ;
No priest nor hooded monk now near thee dwells
To bless the water from thy holy wells.

The ivy o'er thy ruin seems to twine,
As if to guard thy now forsaken shrine ;
Thy roofless walls to chants no more resound,
The birds alone thy choristers are fonnd.

Of old the penitents would wend their way
To thee, in humble faith, on holy day
To meditate, mayhap to join in prayer,
For man and nature well might worship there.

If angels deign'd to camp about thee then,
When in thy aisle was heard the voice of men,
Will they forsake thee now, when thou art known
But as a relic, old and silent grown ?

Will not their harps be hung about this spot
In memory of the saints now long forgot ?
Will not they still, unheard by human ears,
Breathe forth their hymns "in music of the spheres ?"

Will not they linger fondly, even yet,
Among thy stones, with something of regret,
That thou " Thy Sabbaths keeping " may not raise
With them thy pæan to their Maker's praise?

May time deal gently with thy crumbling form,
And save thee from the vandal and the storm ?
May thou, in sweet seclusion ages rise
A fane, still sacred to admiring eyes !

* JESSEMUTH, JESUMOUND, JESMOND.—According to Brand and
Sykes, there was, about 1350, an Hospital here, with a Chapel
dedicated to the Virgin Mary. The ruins of the Chapel may yet
be seen picturesquely situated in the grounds adjoining those of Mr.
George Luckley, the Grove. The shrine of Saint Mary and the holy
well close by were in olden times much esteemed by devotees who
came from all parts of the island. Friday Fields, Jesmond Gardens,
Jesmond Grove, Dene, and Vale, are all parts of a suburb which has
ever been a kind of rural shrine for the people of Newcastle.

THE HOLY WELL, JESMOND GROVE.*

Away from men, in sylvan solitude
 The Holy Well in limpid silence flows ;
Wrapt in sweet nature's own beatitude,
 No other homage now it seeks or knows.

But once it knew the quiet pensive tread
 Of monk or priest on sacred rite intent,
Or weary pilgrim, hither meekly led
 On holy vow or healing virtue bent.

And thus its stream hath flowed from that far time
 When blessed Mary's shrine, in this sweet dell
Took of its liquid wealth for use sublime,
 And made of it indeed, a holy well.

For hither sin-stained feet were wont to draw,
 In search of water from the living well—
Of love and truth, the pure and perfect law,
 Which first from holy lips in Canaan fell.

And even now, may someone here be found,
 In simple pilgrimage of sad regret,
To dip the hand or view the scene around,
 With mem'ries clothed the faithful ne'er forget.

Those steps, once numbered with the creed, 'tis said ;
 Would like Bethesda's pool of old, be sought
By stricken ones, who to the spring were led
 In hopes some miracle might here be wrought.

O time revered ! O halo circled day !
 Whose relics now neglected here we find,
That all thy prestige thus should pass away,
 In pain and sorrow to the pious mind.

May kindly hands be raised to tend the weal
 Of broken cistern and of crumbling shrine,
And by their care for sacred stones reveal,
 Their love and reverence for things divine.

* HOLY WELLS.—One of these wells is about 50 yards up the Grove. It is said once to have had as many steps as there are clauses in the Creed, and is now a wreck. .The other is just below the Chapel ruin.

FRIDAY FIELDS, JESMOND.*

Adieu, dear Friday Fields ! a kind adieu !
Your simple charms will soon be lost to view !
Again, and once again, I'll fondly range
O'er paths whose pleasantness time soon may change,
For modern progress, spreading far and wide,
Sweeps o'er fair nature with resistless tide.
Then let me dwell awhile on what now seems
A fading remnant of my early dreams ;
Enjoying, while I may, ere they depart
For ever from my gaze, though not my heart.
Shall I repine at this, because I've known
And tasted joys and bliss whose sweets are flown?
Or, shall I rather, knowing life's estate,
Submit and drink the bitter cup of fate ?
If so, farewell each path, each tree, and hedge !
A long and last farewell I sadly pledge ;
And though forgotten by the world you be,
An ever faithful heart shall beat in me.

SWEET JESMOND DENE !

O, Jesmond Dene ! sweet Jesmond Dene !
Fair art thou in thy dress of green !
Thy flowery banks and walks between
    Are sylvan beauties, Jesmond Dene.

Thy brook that runs with murmuring sound,
Thy leafy glen so peaceful found,
Thy wells, thy ruin, Jesumound,
    Win hearts to thee, sweet Jesmond Dene.

The bridges that throw o'er thy stream
Their span of rustic arch and beam,
Recall to mind some fairy dream,
    It must be thine, sweet Jesmond Dene.

* These Fields were always a favourite walk in the evenings for young lovers. The entrance to them was by a stile opposite the Moor, and the path went through in front of what is now Burdon Terrace, turning to the left behind the Orphanage, and on between leafy hedges in a narrow footpath to Jesmond Gardens and Jesmond Towers.

Hid in thy bosom stands the mill ;
Whose "race" thy stream was wont to fill ;
I wonder if its wheel goes still,
    With rumbling sound, sweet Jesmond Dene?

Who can resist thy charming Grove,
Where tender hearts delight to rove,
Exchanging there soft vows of love,
    As oft was done, sweet Jesmond Dene?

The flowers that bloom in thy retreat,
The bees that sip their nectar sweet,
The birds that sing, they all repeat—
    That thou art lovely, Jesmond Dene.

THE BRIDGE.*

I've sung the praises of the verdant Dene,
Its wealth of beauty and its peace serene ;
Yet still there is that doth my soul inspire
With grateful joy, if not poetic fire.

I thought how Nature here the earth hath riven,
And then to heal the wound had kindly striven ;
Her storms and torrents cleft the deep ravine,
Her dews and sunshine clothed it o'er with green.

I've stood entranced upon yon slender bridge,
Embosomed among trees on either ridge ;
I've traced the valley's contour sweeping round
From Heaton's banks towards sweet Jesumound.

I feel, indeed, how much we owe the man
Whose gift adorns the vale with graceful span,
From off whose trellised height the eye beholds
Fresh charms in Nature as the view unfolds.

No more the weary foot need climb the brow ;
The fairy scene lies all beneath us now ;
And like the bird when soaring to the sky,
'Twixt earth and heaven we now may sing or sigh.

* Benton Bridge, erected and presented to the City by
Sir William G. Armstrong, C.B.

THE RIPPLING BURN.

"Thy babbling brook that sings its liquid song
In eddying cascades as it flows along."

Along the margin of a stream,
Alone I paced in fancy's dream :
A gentle murm'ring I could hear,
And rippling music struck mine ear.
I listened to the soothing sound,
While birds sang sweetly all around :
A whimp'ring ripple seem'd saying to me,
" Good-bye ! I'm off to the glorious sea."

I knew its home was in the west,
Where dews steal down the mountain's breast ;
Where bleating lambs and wild blue-bells
Meet by the streams from off the fells,
I questioned why it left its home
Of soft green hills, so far to roam :
The whimp'ring ripple seemed saying to me,
" Good-bye ! I'm off to the glorious sea."

I knew the stream below was wide
And madly rushed to swell the tide,
While all above, beyond the hill,
Was safe and calm, and softly still.
I said, " Sweet waters, oh ! restrain
Your onward course, and turn again : "
The whimp'ring ripple seemed saying to me,
" Good-bye ! I'm off to the glorious sea."

I thought, how like to Life this stream ;
Ambition fills each human dream ;
How oft young hearts, though kind and true,
Seek out "fresh fields and pastures new; "
How youthful visions fade away
In blighted hopes and life's decay !—
Then list, ye ripples, oh ! list to me :
Forsake not the hills for the glorious sea.

JESMOND.

The wide expanse that borders on thy west
Sends forth the breeze that gives to life its zest ;
Thy pastures fair, thy valley's soft retreat,
Reveal thy cultured wealth in verdure sweet ;
Thy noble trees, arrayed in foliage green,
Give kindly shelter to thy charms serene ;
Thy rural walks, thy quiet leafy glades,
Are sacred to young hearts when love pervades,
Declining age, too, solace finds in thee
In thoughtful contemplation, " fancy free."
The mind, the eye, here gather rich rewards,
The ear with rapture's filled by songs of birds.
How dull indeed methinks the soul must be,
That beauty and delight finds not in thee !

THAT FIELD OF CORN.

Brightly shines the autumn morn,
Bravely waves the rip'ning corn ;
Shelt'ring trees of changing hue
Cov'ring skies of deep'ning blue :
Bravely waiting to be shorn
Stands my fav'rite field of corn.

Like a stream between its banks,
Like an army's moving ranks,
Each full head a waving plume
Marching boldly to its doom :
Bravely waiting to be shorn
Stands my fav'rite field of corn.

The barley's cut and in the sheaves;
The wheat, like rolling billows, heaves;
The sun looks down with waning power,
All Nature bodes the coming hour :
Still bravely waiting to be shorn
There stands my fav'rite field of corn.

Sandyford, Newcastle, Sept. 1, 1881.

LONELINESS.

In the stillness of evening, when all is so dark,
And nought strikes the ear but the dog's lonely bark ;
When Nature is wrapt in its wintry shroud,
And the snow-covered earth seems to blend with the cloud ;
When the pale lunar Queen, that presides o'er the night,
Wanes in her last quarter, refusing her light ;
When the low sullen sound of the mumuring sea
Comes stealing along, like a whisper, to me ;
Oh! then, in such moments of silence, I own
I feel—yes, I feel— most intensely alone.

SPRING'S EVENING HOUR.

How I love to enjoy spring's evening hour,
When birds carol forth from their leafy bower,
When the zephyr breathes soft through waving trees,
And fragrance from flowers floats on the breeze ;
Then, always then, do I ravish mine ear
With the thrush and the blackbird's notes so clear;
While fluttering songsters, above and around,
In sympathy, warbling choruses sound.
Melodious blackbird ! thy trilling I hear
In rapturous song to thy partner dear,
And echoing harmonies round me swell—
'Tis this makes me love this hour so well !

Newcastle-on-Tyne, 1879.

THE LABURNUMS OF JESMOND.

I know a sweet coppice or two
    Where the clust'ring laburnum grows,
And the lilac of delicate hue,
    And the red and white hawthorn blows.

I own, in the shrubb'ry and park,
    There is many an elegant tree,
But none that elicits remark,
    Like the yellow laburnum from me.

The beech and the chestnut I'm told,
  And the elm are stately to see ;
But give me the green and the gold
  Of the yellow laburnum tree.

Go, walk through my northern bowers,
  Where Jesumond woos the soft breeze
I challenge the fairest of flowers
  To rival laburnums like these.

Sandyford, 1881.

THE MEADOW.

There is a meadow, fresh and green,
  Near by a shady lane :
To see that meadow oft I've been,
  And oft would go again.

Each blade of grass that's growing there
  And each outspreading tree,
And all that makes that meadow fair
  Seems like old friends to me.

The happy birds, whose swelling notes
  Float softly on the breeze,
Seem there to tune their little throats
  More ardently to please.

The sun seems brighter beams to cast,
  To make that meadow fair :
Oh ! could its beauty always last,
  My heart would aye be there.

Then, linger there, sweet verdant Spring ;
  New life is in thy arms ;
And I my choicest songs will sing,
  And praise my meadow's charms.

Jesmond, June 1st, 1881.

SWEET MEMORIES.

I love the shady lane,
  With sunbeams shining through,
The lark's sweet, clear refrain,
  In skies both bright and blue.

I love the moss-grown seat
  Beneath the leafy hedge,
Where I my love did meet,
  Our mutual love to pledge.

I love to feel again,
  Through memory's tender chord,
What of those joys remain,
  Of look, or smile, or word.

Come, dear one, to my heart,
  And make those memories real ;
No more again to part,
  But deeper joys to feel.

THE KING OF JESMOND.

I grew from simple youth's romantic hour
To full maturity's ripe age and power.
My days till then seemed all one happy dream ;
Life's wish achieved, I reigned a King supreme.

In regal pride I gazed on all around,
In strength and stature rivals none I found ;
Complacently I dwelt, my title own'd,
Born thus to rule, a King I sate enthroned.

Like other monarchs, I rejoiced in power,
And on life's changing stage did " strut mine hour,"
Empires might rise, " decline and fall," 'twould seem ;
Mine was exempt, for here I reigned supreme.

But death has come to me, as 'twill to all,
And pomp and power is tott'ring to its fall :
Prepare ye cypress, then my grave to deck,
I, King of Jesmond, am to-day a wreck.

A century has cycled o'er this dene
Since first my sapling graced its wild ravine ;
The monks are gone, the pilgrims come no more,
And now the reign of Jesmond's King is o'er.

THE DEATH OF THE ASH TREE.*

(KNOWN AS THE KING OF JESMOND.)

The Ash, the monarch of the vale,
    Whose giant form hath been,
Through summer's heat and winter's gale,
    The King of Jesmond Dene;
Whose mighty stem for years and years
    Hath reared its lofty head,
Outliving human hopes and fears,
    This King of Jesmond's dead.

The birds have found in him a staunch
    And ever friendly aid,
They nestled safely on his branch
    And sang beneath his shade;
But now their choicest notes they'll quell,
    And sing a dirge instead,
In plaintive tones they'll sadly tell,
    The King of Jesmond's dead.

* This was a large ash tree which stood at the corner of the road close by Jesmond Gardens. It was supposed by some to be over 150 years old ; and about 60 feet high. Its girth round the trunk, at one yard from the ground, was 15 feet. From its size and position it received the name of the King of Jesmond, and in its halcyon days when in full foliage, and made musical by the swarms of bees which occasionally hived in its stem, must have well deserved the title.

The holy wells whose limpid flow
  Have been the pilgrim's cheer,
Will murmur requiems soft and low
  When they the tidings hear.
The springs their sympathy will yield,
  And trickling teardrops shed,
And tell each sunny bank and field
  The King of Jesmond's dead.

The flowers that in the autumn bloomed,
  By winter lulled to sleep,
Wot not their noble king was doomed
  Ere they from earth should peep.
As each awoke to vernal skies,
  And raised its pearly head,
It heard with dewdrops in its eyes
  The King of Jesmond's dead.

The monarch gazed with saddened glance,
  When last he budded forth,
He saw the mighty town advance
  To claim his place of birth.
Down from his height on puny man
  He looked with wounded pride ;
Answered, as only greatness can,
  Bloomed once again, and died.

THE DEAD ASH TREE.

Oh, how I long a farewell dirge to sing ;
The King of Jesmond's dead ! " Long live the King,"
The brave ash monarch, whose ambrosial sway
Trends back for centuries, now meets decay.

His topmost branches kissed the western gale,
His roots struck deeply in the sloping vale,
He heard the booming of the world's great tide
Advancing on him, shed his leaves, and died.

Weep tears of sorrow, O ! ye holy wells,
Let dewdrops stain your cheeks, ye leafy dells ;
Let tones of sadness through your warblings ring,
Ye feathered songsters, while ye mourn your King.

" Hang out no banners," O, ye Jesmond Towers,
Grow wreaths of cypress, O, ye Jesmond bowers,
Ye lofty sycamores raise not a head,
But droop in wailing, for your King is dead.

Look up, ye pigmies of the human race !
Behold this patriarch, then hide your face,
Think of his greatness while his wreck you scan,
Then, of the littleness of fleeting man.

May 3rd, 1880.

A NOBLE DOMAIN.

"Truly the light is sweet, and a pleasant thing it is for the eyes
to behold the sun."—ECCLES. xi., 7.

I have a domain which is all my own ;
  'Tis the gift of the Giver of light :
A gift that is not unto me alone,
  But to all who are blessed with sight.

And in it are mountains and valleys and streams,
  And flowers, and forests of trees,
And landscapes illumined with heaven's bright beams ;
  And I am the owner of these.

And though not a rood of this land I may sell,
  Yet still its enjoyment is mine ;
And not only mine, but 'tis yours as well,
  If with love you contentment combine.

And the charter that gives me this noble domain
  Is the marvellous power of sight ;
And this is the gift, let me say it again,
  Of the Father of goodness and light.

JESMOND DENE IN AUTUMN.

Dear Jesmond ! in thy sheltered vale,
Where birds the listening ear regale,
I fondly stray with deep delight
As autumn's sunbeams wane in night ;
The leaves are changing quickly then,
And strew the pathways in thy glen,
The fading verdure all around
Will soon in nature's sleep be found,
Though lingering spots of brighter green
Contrast and lighten up the scene.
Dear valley ! though unknown to fame
By noble deed, or classic name,
A simpler wreath than laurel bough—
Our love—adorns thy placid brow,
There may be other lands more fair,
With bluer skies and softer air ;
But few there are with charms, I ween,
That equal thine, sweet Jesmond Dene.

JESMOND GROVE IN WINTER.

I love thee in the winter time,
    When thou art clad in snow ;
When trees and leaves with frosted rime
    In glistening spangles show.

When Christmas, stern December's king,
    Rules over all below ;
And bids them holly branches bring
    And festive mistletoe.

Then do I love to walk abroad,
    And tread, with joyous feet,
Thy crispy paths, whose frost-bound road
    Speaks back in music sweet.

Then robins sing their warbling song,
    As if our hearts to cheer ;
For winter may not tarry long,
    And spring will soon be here.

Christmas Day, 188c.   B

'TIS SPRING TO DAY.

The sun was warm, and mellow was the air,
And Spring was come, and all was bright and fair;
I wandered in the grove close by the dene,
Where nature is displayed in freshest green.

Beside an aged ruin, on a tree
I saw the thrush chant forth his melody;
In trilling notes my fancy heard him say—
" Mortal, be happy; it is Spring to-day!"

I listened, as he perched the leaves among;
And, as I listened, oh! how sweet his song;
Yet still his warblings ever seemed to say—
" Mortal, be happy; it is Spring to day!"

And on I wandered through the vale's retreat,
The blackbird there was singing loud and sweet;
And, like his rival too, he seemed to say—
" Mortal, be happy; it is Spring to-day!"

I mused on this, both earnestly and long;
Why should it be the theme of feathered song?
Why mortals only silent homage pay,
While birds sing joyfully, "'Tis Spring to-day?"

God's gifts to us are many more than theirs;
They've neither barn nor storehouse, wheat nor tares;
Yet are they first the joyous news to bring,
And sing the praises of the hopeful Spring.

'Tis Hope " that springs eternal in the breast,"
'Tis this that makes the songbirds' theme the best;
Bright days are coming, and the songs they sing
Prove them the harbingers of welcome Spring!

THE CEMETERY : HER GRAVE.

―――

"Some loved ones lie on the breezy slopes
Of sunlit hills with our buried hopes;
Some in the sea, or in cavern rude,
But here in a sylvan solitude "

―――

I've been to see the grave wherein she lies
    In death's cold silence in her narrow bed,
Watched only by the never-slumb'ring eyes
    That keep the vigils o'er the sleeping dead.

I've been to see the flow'rs whose faded bloom,
    Though cherished for her sake, no art could save ;
Sweet emblems of herself in that dark tomb,
    They woo me oft to linger by her grave.

I stand and gaze upon the earthy shroud,
    And wonder if she knows that I am near,
While o'er it, as I bend with sorrow bowed,
    I seek relief in many a sigh and tear.

I long to tell her all I think and feel,
    How much I miss her from my home and side ;
How time and distance never more shall heal
    The wound which only death alone can hide.

Oh ! could it be that she again might smile
    Or whisper in my ear one loving word,
It would so soothe this aching heart the while,
    And wake within me many a tender chord.

Yes, there in that cold grave she calmly lies,
    And I, alas ! must tear myself away
To seek in hope what mem'ry now denies,
    And wait the union of eternal day.

ST. JAMES'S, NEWCASTLE.*

Farewell, St. James's ! from thy terraced brow
No more wilt thou thy peaceful shadow throw ;
Thy modest front, which often met our eyes,
Will disappear amid regrets and sighs.

Another pile of more pretentious name
Will take thy place to win a nobler fame ;
But there are some who'll love thee to the last,
Not for thy beauty, but for mem'ries past.

Oft at the opening of the vernal year
Thy missel-thrush hath charmed and soothed mine ear;
Oft 'neath the heat of summer's sultry sky
Thy leafy verdure hath refreshed mine eye.

Once more, sweet warbler, let me hear thy song;
Repeat thy cadences, 'twill not be long
Ere thou and thine, now safely nestling near,
Will, like myself, have naught to bind thee here.

Oft 'neath the silent silver crescent moon
I've watched the waning day close in too soon,
While to the murmur of thy waving trees
I've quaffed delicious perfumes from the breeze.

Sad is my heart (but sadness is our lot),
As one by one I miss each much-loved spot;
And see with tearful eye fair nature's face
Robbed of those features we can ne'er replace.

" A thing of beauty is a joy for ever,"
Then from the beautiful, O part us never !
But win us from the world's debasing arms
By wooing us through nature's softer charms !

Newcastle, April, 1880.

* The building above referred to was pulled down in April, 1880,
to make way for the Natural History Society's Museum.   In ancient
times there was a chapel of St. James's in the neighbourhood, from
which it probably took its name.   The grounds behind the house
were every season visited by the thrush, whose rich and pleasing
notes attracted the attention of passers by.

ST. NICHOLAS'S CHIMES.

St. Nicholas ! thy chimes I love,
As they sound from thy spire above ;
Their mellow tones float on the air
As if the cloistered monks were there ;
And still amid these changing times
I love to hear thy pleasant chimes !

Thy sacred fane points to the sky,
Rich in the mem'ries of long bye !
And ever in the world's great din
Thou bid'st us seek the " peace within."
And still amid these changing times
I love to hear thy pleasant chimes !

Thy bells ring in the Christmas morn,
And welcome in the year new-born,
And when its waning days have roll'd
Its death upon thy bell is toll'd !
And still amid these changing times
I love to hear thy pleasant chimes !

Newcastle-on-Tyne, Christmas, 1880.

OUR ANCIENT WALLS.

" Fortiter Defendit Triumphans."

Long years gone by when Roman feet
Bade Briton's isle farewell,
Leaving to barriers, camps, and roads
Of centuries' rule to tell—
When Danish kings had passed away,
And Pict and Scot o'erran
Both Offa's Dyke and Hadrian's wall—
Then Saxon rule began ;
But Celtic raids and feudal wars,
And conquering Norman bands,
Crushed for a while the nation's strength,
And wasted homes and lands :

Till British, Saxon, Norman blood
   Blent, on Northumbria's soil
Raised for themselves protecting walls
   With patient hope and toil ;
Taught by that noble Roman work,
   From Solway to the Tyne,
The latent strength that nature yields
   When art and will combine ;
Then fickle peace awhile would reign,
   And, freed from wars' alarms,
They'd moulded be to gentler life,
   Till called afresh to arms.
"Alarm ! alarm ! sound the alarm—
   Sound, ere it be too late ;
Mount Castle, Tower, and Rampart—
   Guard every fortress gate ;
Send horsemen forth by Neville's Cross
   The western hills to scour ;
Man turrets, walls, and battlements,
   From Pink to Carliol's Tower ;
Let sword and spear be girded on,
   Let trench and moat be filled—
To arms ! ye Novocastrians,
   Both merchantmen and guild ! "
Soon clash and clang of warrior
   Would angrily resound,
And friend with foe be struggling
   In mortal strife around,
While women's tears and children's cries
   Would rend the hearts of all,
As they beheld the opening breach
   Grow wider in the wall ;
But hearths and homes the brave make strong,
   So with a rallying shout
They'd fling themselves the foe upon
   And fiercely drive them out ;
Thus nobly did our ancestors
   Respond to duty's call,
Bequeathing us their freedom,
   Their fame, their towers, and wall.

Revolving years bring round events,
 And by an adverse fate
Again we're called the foe to meet—
 An enemy's at the gate ;
This time-worn relic of the past—
 Our history writ in stone—
Is doomed by rash Iconoclasts
 In spite of many a groan :
Unheeded too are earnest prayers
 From patriot and from friend,
Whose honoured names and generous deeds
 Should every wish commend ;
But vain ambition, unrestrained,
 Stays not to count the cost,
And that its object may be gained
 A landmark may be lost ;
But we will plead no more with them—
 The vandals of to-day ;
Like Goths and Huns they'll be contemned,
 And like them pass away.

March, 1879.

THE TOWER'S APPEAL.

"Go round about her . . . tell the Towers thereof."

Oh Novocastrians ! in your infant days
I and my brethren guarded all your ways ;
And, as in youth you spread from hill to hill,
We then preserved and would preserve you still.
Each stone in us was laid with patient toil
By men who bore the sword, yet loved the soil ;
Whom oft I've seen, when roused by war's alarms,
Rush quick to muster in our sheltering arms ;
Then sally forth to meet the invading foe,
And deal to Scot or Dane a deadly blow.
Then, peace regained, my battlements have seen
Their simple mirth in Pandon's sylvan dene.

The ancient Castle which your title gives—
Chief Monarch of our tribe—still bravely lives;
Your steeple, too, whose architectural crown,
In silent majesty adorns your town;
These both, I know, are held in great regard,
And, in your care, possess a rich reward;
With them I watch and ward have sternly kept
While safe within the fold your children slept.

Shall I recount, from history's crowded page,
The names and deeds renowned in every age
Of those whose fame threw lustre on your Wall,
In which I claim some share, though it be small?
'Twould need a " Bruce's " wealth of Roman lore,
With power to summon " Cohorts " to my door,
That I might point to them, for witness true,
How much your Walls and Towers have won for you.

Alas! though Learning, Art, and Science all agree
That there may still be found some worth in me,
Yet there are men, whom you have raised to power,
Who thirst to lay in dust your CARLIOL TOWER!

THE TOWER'S WARNING.

The sun has set on the battle; our warriors faint and
 few
Have fought while day was with them.   The sword no
 more can do.
If the conquering foe be generous, to him we'll proudly
 kneel,
But noble hearts would rather die than to a tyrant
 yield;
Beware then, " Sons of Belial," hands off our Carliol
 Tower!
Remember if the day be yours, there comes a reckoning
 hour;
And, though ye may enshrine yourselves within a stately
 hall,
The stigma of ingratitude shall cling around you all!

THE DEMOLITION OF THE CARLIOL TOWER.*

O ! Ancient Tower ! by thy fate we read
A lesson that the best of us may need —
That age and worth, though they may claim respect,
Are much too often served with chill neglect.
Thy enemies were strong, relentless, bold ;
The hearts that knew and loved thee, all were cold ;
The hands that might have saved thee from this fate
Were palsied with the gloss of " Roman " state.
How dead the sentiment ! how poor the style !
That sacrifices thee, O hoary pile !
To false expediency's repulsive claim,
A public loss to win a paltry fame.
Children unborn will live to curse the day—
And them—that bid thy walls be swept away.

Newcastle, April, 28, 1880.

THE TYNE.

Three streams upon one mountain range arise—
The offspring of fair Cumbria's cloud-capp'd hills
Where winter's snowy mantle lingering lies
Till freed by spring's warm breath to fill the rills—
There, like three neighbours' children, born and bred
Upon the same hillside, to life they start,
Nursed on the same green breast, together fed
They yet seek out a course that's far apart.

" I seek the birthplace of a native stream,"
'Tis thee, O Tyne then, that shall be my theme
With thy twin waters, both of north and south
That blend in one grand flood down to thy mouth.

* The picturesque tower, around whose site was waged the battle
of the Public Library Buildings, was taken down in April, 1880. It
seems almost a crime to denude this old border town of its ancient
landmarks, and to rob future generations of the privilege of contemplating and admiring that which new countries with no history would
treasure as priceless relics.

O Tyne ! thou art indeed Northumbria's river,
Thy swelling stream flows on majestic ever;
But here, beneath fair Warden's wooded hill,
The meeting of thy waters hold me still ;
Whence let me view thee o'er thy wondrous course,
Down from thy moorland home and mountain source;
There, to the south, far up yon breezy fells
Th' adventurous miner in his sheeling dwells,
With lonely toil his skilful force he wields
Until the hidden vein its treasure yields.
There man hath yoked fair nature, and his team
He finds in many a gorge-pent mountain stream,
And heathery moors invite the sturdy frame
Of sportsman eager for the wingèd game.

From these I turn towards thy northern flood,
With all its moorland charms of vale and wood;
Its feudal castles and its peels and towers,
Its wild morasses and its glens and bowers ;
Its rude mosstroopers and its border frays,
Its men and manners of long gone-by days,
That bards have sung of and historians told
In tales and incidents of days of old.   .
'Tis these I'd sing of, but thy pregnant streams
O'erwhelm me with their rich and varied themes;
Yea, I would rather dwell on days benign
That peace hath bless'd thee with, O " Coaly Tyne."

How fitly art thou named, O Tynedale's stream !
For thy " black diamonds " cast a ray supreme
O'er all thy fortunes, and thy native fame
Lives ever in thy " Wallsend's " homely name.
These are the gems that deck thy river-god,
For Roman, Saxon, Norman feet have trod
Thy fortress'd banks, whose battlements preside
O'er fleets of argosies that stem thy tide.

" Pons Ælii ! thou treasured Roman gem,"
And relique of the Norman's diadem;
Thy heirs have won for thee a worthy name,
And for themselves a never dying fame.

In learning, art, invention, science, skill,
They each a lengthening scroll in history fill;
Thy Armstrong, Stephenson, and Collingwood
Were giants and the nurslings of thy flood.
" And nature, too, thy stream hath so endowed
With gifts of which thy sons may well be proud,"
For many a sylvan dell and sacred fane
In sweet sequestered beauty yet remain ;
Though as I trace thy stream from mouth to source
Predominant I find material force ;
The signal sounds, and from their couches spring
The legions of some great industrial king,
While from their busy hives incessant team
The products of hydraulic force and steam,
Which from thy pier-girt mouth with every breeze,
Go forth to bear thy fame across the seas.

SALTWELL PARK.

I wandered by Elysium Lane,
To Saltwell's lovely park ;
Delights are there in endless train,
Which memory loves to mark.

O ! charming valley of the Team,
Thy beauty stands confessed ;
Before thy terraced slopes there gleam
Bright visions of the west.

From Bensham's sunny bank is seen
Old Tyne in all its pride,
While Nature in her freshest green,
Sweeps down towards its tide.

Bold Sheriff Hill and Gateshead's Fells,
With steeple standing high,
While wooded Ravensworth's green dells
Swell upwards to the sky.

The sylvan glen, the trickling stream,
  Where rustic bridges span
From bank to bank, make Saltwell seem
  A Paradise for man.

Its flowery beds, its meadows green,
  Its paths and leafy shades,
Its winding maze, its fairy dene
  Form here perennial glades.

Ye weary denizens who toil,
  Come, visit Nature's home ;
She wears for you her fairest smile,
  And sweetly bids you come.

Whoe'er they be, whate'er their name,
  Who won this for their town,
Have mantled Gateshead with a fame
  Which clothes them with renown !

Newcastle, July, 1880.

CROFT HOUSE, OVINGHAM.

DEDICATED TO ALEXANDER WOOD, ESQ.

Ye banks of Tyne ! where falls the Whittle Dene,
And sleeps old Ovingham in peace serene ;
Washed are your borders by Tyne's rippling wave,
And hallowed as the home of Bewick's grave.

Here time with gentle motion onward flows,
And nature dreams in rustic calm repose ;
While past and present both their treasures blend
In loving rivalry some charm to lend.

For here the Roman and his *vallum'd* wall,
The rude Mosstrooper and his border hall,—
The lordly Baron and his castled height,
All join to yield a weird and bygone light.

But peace and righteousness, now hand-in-hand,
Have changed the face of this historic land ;
And spots that once the lawless foot oppress'd,
Are now the wearied merchant's welcome rest.

BYWELL.

O Bywell! sweet Bywell! by Tyne's flowing stream,
 Thy wealth of green woodlands are charming to see;
Amid thy surroundings I thoughtfully dream,
 And gaze on the beauty, unrivall'd, in thee.

Thou gem of fair Tynedale, whose smooth rocky breast
 Is worn by the force of the flood-driven waves,
Thy sylvan seclusion invites me to rest
 Where the murmuring waters sound over thy graves.

Around thy twin churches I silently tread,
 And muse o'er their relics of earlier days,
As I mark how they gather around them the dead,
 I hear living voices uplifted in praise.

I gaze on thy ivy-clad Castle's decay,
 And grieve that its martial renown should e'er cease;
But if power and prestige must vanish away,
 I will love its old walls in their mantle of peace.

O Bywell! the treasures that cluster thy vale,
 Find picturesque form and expression in thee;
Each historic incident, relic and tale,
 Speak a language of eloquent meaning to me.

BYWELL CASTLE.

TO JOHN HALL, ESQ.

O Bywell Castle! stern and old,
 There's romance in thy rugged form;
Couldst thou but speak thou mightst unfold,
 Grim tales of battle, flood and storm.

The Umfreville's and Neville's brave,
 Are linked in story with thy walls;
They now lie silent in the grave,
 While gentler hearts beat in thy halls.

Thy battlements must oft have seen
The must'ring ranks march out afar,
Thy rude oak gates must oft have been
Swung to and fro in pomp or war.

No more thy henchman need to guard
The cattle folded in thy street,
Nor sentinels keep watch and ward
The riever and the foe to meet.

For peace now in thee, Bywell, dwells,
And wealth its charm around thee throws ;
But oh ! the sweetest of thy spells,
Is thy soft beauty and repose.

THE GRAND OLD ENGLISH FAIR.*

Ye Proclamation of ye Fayre.

It was ye custome in ye olden time,
To sette forth historie in ye quaintest rhyme;
Ye Minstrel sang ye doings of eache plaice,
Ye foraye, or ye trystinge, or ye chase.
So we proclaime herein withe alle due care,
Ye openinge of ye Grand Olde Englishe Fayre.

O Yes ! O Yes ! O Yes !

To alle and everie we declare,
Ye openinge of our Englyshe Fayre,
To whyche we hereby do invite,
Ye Ladye Fayre, and gallant Knight;
Ye Merchant from ye busy Quay,
Ye Captaine too, freshe home from sea ;
Ye Maister-man of everie trade,
Ye workers too of everie grade
That builde greete Ships, or dig ye Mine,
And win muche wealthe for Father Tyne.

* Written for the Grand Old English Fair, held in the Town Hall,
Newcastle, October, 1883, in aid of the Northumberland Village
Homes, Whitley-by-the-Sea, which was very successful, realising,
after deducting expenses, the handsome net sum of £4,000.

Come neighboures alle and be not dulle,
Each wythe your pouche well lined and fulle,
Of Goulden Guineas a goodlie store,
Whyche when welle spent goe bring you more ;
For Laydies fayre wythe smiles full sweet,
Are waiteing there eache one to greete,
With winninge looke and laughing eye,
To tempt you some nice thinge to buy ;
Mayhap a bracelet for ye ladye's arme,
Or cosie nice to keepe ye tea potte warme ;
Or slippers dight all o'er wythe beades so neate,
To give ye olde dame for her goode man's feete;
Or new cravatte or choker for Papa,
Or gloves or farthingale for deare Mama;
Or little sockes or shoes for babie boy,
Or balle or hoope or some such toy,
Or, cozened by ye deare one atte your side,
Ye purchase somethinge for ye soon-he bride;
But whatsoe'er ye thinge or price may be,
Pull out your pouche and pay ye maiden's fee,
For gentle hands have made ye goodes that's there,
And Cheerful Charitie delights ye fayre.

YE SEQUELLE TO YE FAYRE.

Ye Fayre is ended and ye stalles are closed,
And all ye merchandize is now disposed;
Ye ladies fayre and gallant men who stood
Within ye Market Plaice, are gone for good;
And alle ye noble souls who strove their best
In love's great traffick, now have welle won rest.
Ye buyers too, of high and low degree,
That came to see, and spend so lib'ralie,
And parted braivelie wythe their hard-earned gold,
Are now welle pleased that they were "bought and sold."
These alle have gone welle laden from ye Fayre :
Each to hys home and left ye stalles quite bare ;
And while ye sellers rest them from their toils,
Ye buyers will displaie wythe pride their spoils.

But see now ! sitting round ye festive board,
Ye whilome merchants, gloating o'er their hoard
Of welle won thousands, and re-telling o'er
Their tussels atte eache raffle, stalle, and store,
How alle their smiles and coaxing failed to make
Some old curmudgeon one cheap " lot " to take;
And while atte times they strove to vende their stuffe
They blandly had to bear with sharp rebuffe.
How one would chaffer and then change hys minde,
Say " Things are dear, no bargains could he finde,"
And then goe try hys luck down in ye " Welle,"
And atte ye bottom finde ye truth a " Selle."
Then to ye stalles again return wythe smiles
To fall a victim to more cunninge wyles.

How artfullie they strove their hooks to bait,
And for ye purchasers did watchfulle wait;
What goodlie sorte did fall into their snares
Who noblie spent their cashe and bought their wares;
And, laughinglie they'll telle, how, wythe a grin,
Some poor wight came untoe ye " Tabard Inne,"
And ordered for himself a humble " drain,"
But stared to finde hys bill was for champagne.

How all, amid ye din and heat they stoode,
Sustainèd by ye thowt of doing goode.
How eache new sale effected atte ye store
But spurr'd them on to try and selle ye more.
They'll laugh to think, their handes for pleasure made,
So deftlie fell unto ye knack of " trade."
'Twas but for four short days ye Fayre did last,
But months of thought and toil in them were cast,
For gentle hands, both willinglie and welle,
Had laboured hard to furnish goodes to selle.
And gen'rous hearts did braivelie give and spende,
So wythe success our " Englyshe Fayre " did end.

    ✲   *   *   ✲   ✲

But hark! What is this? A sweet chorus I hear—
'Tis the soft voice of childhood that rings in mine ear;
'Tis a song of thanksgiving from Homes by the sea,
From hearts full of gladness, to you and to me;
And its sound shall be echoed,from streets sorrow-paved,
From the lips of our sad little waifs to be saved.
'Tis their thanks for the labour and wealth you have given
That shall find a re-echo from angels in heaven.

ON THE SILVER WEDDING OF MR. AND MRS. JAMES HALL,

TYNEMOUTH, NORTHUMBERLAND.

O Welcome Day! the dawn of which imparts
A new yet old emotion to your hearts,
Reviving memories of a time long past,
O'erflowing with life's joys too sweet to last.

Yes, five-and-twenty years have pass'd away
In loving union since that happy day,
When in the sacred link of wedlock's chain
Your lives were bound in one, aye to remain.

How full of Christian work those years have been
The Industrial Dwellings show, as we have seen;
The "Village Homes" and "Wellesley" proclaim
That hosts of children yet shall bless your name.

Bless'd in each other and the world's regard
You've won from grateful hearts a proud reward;
The path of duty which you've nobly trod
Has bloomed beneath your steps with fruits to God.

May He who gave you grace, and wealth, and power,
To help the helpless in their darkest hour,
So give you friends to love you and to pray
For blessings on your Silver Wedding Day.

February 10th, 1888.

C

THE GOLDEN WEDDING DAY

OF

THE REV. DR. J. COLLINGWOOD BRUCE,

AND MRS. BRUCE,

June 20th, 1883.

All hail ! dear Doctor, we rejoice to pay
Our welcome on thy Golden Nuptial Day,
Which binds anew two lives, whose hopes and fears
Now hold their Jubilee of wedded years.

Bless'd hast thou been in health and length of days;
Time hath adorned thee with its choicest bays—
A wreath of well-spent years, the honoured crown,
Of life-long labours gilded with renown.

Thy gifts of culture and thy learned fame,
Unite to throw a lustre round thy name;
On Roman Britain's storied-page sublime
Thou'lt leave thy "footprints on the sands of time."

O ! Sage and Christian ! Christian more than sage,
Beloved of youth, still more revered by age,
May thou and thy dear helpmeet, hand in hand,
Be gently led towards the Better Land.

May Heaven around thy pathway never cease
To cast the cheering rays of joy and peace ;
As thou hast sown in deeds of Christian love,
May it be thine to reap in realms above.

TO THE WANSBECK.

" O ye Northumbrian shades, which overlook
The rocky pavement and the mossy falls
Of solitary Wansbeck's limpid stream."—*Akenside.*

Flow on, brown Wansbeck, to the Northern Sea,
Whose waves at Cambois Bay will welcome thee :
Flow on, thou maiden of the moorland mist,
By many a leafy glen and wildflower kiss'd.

No more thy stream shall see its dewy home ;
Far from its mountain slopes 'tis doomed to roam ;
And as it swells beneath the dropping skies
'Twill murmur to its banks some soft good-byes.

Thou offspring of the hills ! whose grassy sod
Knows but the shepherd's staff and fisher's rod,
Ambition's floods may tempt thee to the main,
But Sweethope's Loughs thou ne'er wilt see again.

But who can tell what Fate may have in store
For thee and sister Blyth, whose links-clad shore
Waits but for Enterprise to lift her hand,
To spring to fame, and fortune to command?

Newcastle, March, 1881.

TYNEMOUTH—A LAMENT.

AIR: "The Meeting of the Waters."

O ! the cliffs of old Tynemouth are ragged and worn,
And the Haven's green banks of their beauty are shorn,
Yet our dear ancient Priory that stands by the sea,
Though the spot of the wild winds, is still dear to me.

O ! touch not the churchyard that shelters the dead,
Nor remove the old gravestones that mark where they're
    laid ;
Nay, watch o'er each relic whose presence now lends
A charm to the mem'ry of long-buried friends.

O ! guard those dear cliffs that environ our shore,
For we cling to them still as we loved them of yore ;
To all dangers that threaten a bold front we'll show,
And their picturesque beauty defend from the foe.

In the days of our childhood we wander'd at will
O'er the beach and its crags and each grass-covered hill :
And we still in old age love to gaze "fancy free"
From thy cliffs, dear old Tynemouth, across the blue sea.

Newcastle, 1887.

THE TRIUMPHS OF PEACE.

The nations may boast of their warriors bold,
　And their battles and conquests by land and by sea ;
They may point to the page where their glory is told,
　And the trophies they've won from the brave and the free;
But the spears of their heroes now lie in the dust,
　And their helmets and banners no longer do shine,
But we seek for the fame of the right and the just,
　So the triumphs of peace gild the banks of old Tyne.

The fleets of old England all over are seen,
　Though more often in pomp than the carnage of war,
Wherever they be they declare her the queen
　Over commerce and art, which is better by far.
But more mightier conquests by her have been won
　Through the force of her skill in the workshop and mine;
For she seeks not to rule by the sabre and gun,
　So the triumphs of peace gild the banks of old Tyne.

From thy dear cliffs, old Tynemouth, we gaze o'er the sea,
　And behold the proud river that flows at our feet ;
And we think of the manhood so gallant and free
　That in friendship and love in her havens we meet ;
And we think of the dear ones so loving and fair
　That enthrall'd our young hearts with a passion divine;
And we feel it is true as we breathe her fresh air,
　That the triumphs of peace gild the banks of old Tyne.

CROXDALE GLEN.

O Croxdale Glen ! O Croxdale Glen !
So little known to mortal ken ;
But half revealed by writer's pen,
I'll sing of thee, sweet Croxdale glen.

Thy road so steep, thy bridge so old,
Thy clust'ring trees, thy cliffs so bold,
Thy gorge so deep, thy waters cold,
Are gems of thine, sweet Croxdale glen.

Within thy glen so softly still,
No sound was heard but of thy mill,
Thy splashing wheel, thy water rill,
But they were music, Croxdale glen.

The lovely maid who graced thy dell,
The mill in which she deigned to dwell,
The swain that came, his love to tell,
Gave life to thee, sweet Croxdale glen.

The evenings spent within thy grove,
As in communion sweet they'd rove,
His simple tale of earnest love,
Were known to thee, sweet Croxdale glen.

"Rough stones do fret the limpid burn ;
The sweetest rose must bear its thorn,
And hearts by jealous thoughts are torn,"
So with thy swain, sweet Croxdale glen.

From Durham's ancient city went
A foppish youth on love intent ;
A while her ear the maiden lent
As woman will, sweet Croxdale glen.

By this vain youth a scheme was laid
To force from thee thy gentle maid,
For which with life he nearly paid
In thy dark stream, sweet Croxdale glen.

But fortune ever with the brave,
Brought loving swain in time to save
Her from the youth, him from a grave
Beneath thy bridge, sweet Croxdale glen.

The fiery steed that dashed away
With driver false, on that rough way,
No doubt its life it had to pay ;
But hers was spared, sweet Croxdale glen.

Oh, noble heart of faithful swain,
That could so soon forgive again,
And strive to save with might and main
Him who would rob thee, Croxdale glen.

And as the youth in safety stood
And glanced beneath at thy dark flood,
His heart was changed ; in thankful mood
He blessed thy swain, sweet Croxdale glen.

What stays thee, O thou splashing wheel?
What stills thy sound, O rumbling mill?
To-day thy swain's true heart will fill,
Thy maid's his wife, sweet Croxdale glen.

Newcastle-on-Tyne, Sept. 1879.

JOHN STOREY.

What name shall fame to memory bring
With Richardson's through time to ring,
Who drank in youth the same art spring ?
John Storey.

Who made the colours at command
To glow beneath his master hand
In scenes of home both true and grand ?
John Storey.

Who limned us many an ancient spot
That link'd us with the Pict and Scot,
With others not to be forgot ?
John Storey.

Who won himself and us renown,
And o'er his works raised these the crown
Our " Ancient " and our " Modern " town ?
John Storey.

Whom did the " mantle " fall upon
Of Richardson when he was gone,
Who has the master's hand outshone ?
John Storey.

Who lives in many a work of art ?
Who lives in many a friendly heart ?
Who leaves a gap whene'er we part ?
John Storey.

THE MILLER OF ALLERSTON.

INSCRIBED TO MR. WILLIAM WARD.

In a fair spreading valley not far from the sea,
Dwells the Miller of Allerston, jovial and free ;
There's a joy in my heart that dear Ebberston yields,
That is crowned by the verdure of Yeddingham's fields.

Flow on, gentle waters ! flow on to the Mill,
Bid the daughters of Allerston think of me still ;
Say to Annie and Elise, its maidens so fair,
That my heart's ever yearning again to be there.

O turn thee, then, water-wheel cheerfully round,
There is music to me in thy rhythmical sound ;
The reapers are reaping in yon sunny plain,
And will send thee rich harvests of ripe golden grain.

Farewell to thy charms, then, dear Allerston Mill,
Though I leave thee, my heart shall remain with thee still ;
While the Derwent's cool stream seeks its way to the sea,
Thy Mill and the Miller remembered shall be.

Sept. 18th, 1885.

A CENTENARY HYMN.

See the children bravely thronging,
    Sunday scholars, Christian lambs,
Each to some good fold belonging,
    Marching with their hymns and psalms !

Bid them come, with banners flying,
    Thousands in one company,
Ignorance and sin defying,
    One on high says, " Come to me."

Blessings on the noble teachers,
    Who their willing labours give,
To transform their fellow creatures,
    And to teach them how to live !

Newcastle, July, 1880.

THE POET'S FRIENDS.*

A poet once in Novocastria dwelt,
Who sometimes scraps of metre rudely spelt ;
His talent might have died without a name,
Had not the *Advertiser* fed the flame.

Take heart then, humble lovers of the Muse,
And when the Graces hint, do not refuse ;
Some kindly heart may lend a helping hand
To bear thee on towards thy "promised land."

Perhaps there may arise a Robert Ward,
To guide thy footsteps with a friendly guard ;
A Dickson, or a Hastings, now and then
May help thy feeble flight with ready pen.

A Haggerston or Chater may in need
Speed on the wings of thy Pegasian steed ;
A friend like Heppell, too, thou e'en might find,
With facile pen and quaint but well-stored mind.

There may be Allans, too, with hearts to give
A brother's hand to help thy Muse to live ;
For poets are like moths around a flame,
Too often finding death while seeking fame.

These are the friends towards whom memory turns ;
They claim this meed of thanks while life's lamp burns ;
'Tis little, yet 'tis much, in this regard—
'Tis as the widow's mite from Jesmond's Bard.

* This "acknowledgment for past favours," as Mr. Horsley him-
self terms it, was inserted in the last issue of the *North of England
Advertiser*, October 18, 1884. Mr. Robert Ward, here mentioned, was
the proprietor and publisher of the *North of England Advertiser*, and
Ward's Directory, with whom Mr. Horsley was so long connected ; Mr.
Wm. Dickson was the editor of that paper, and the writer of the " Lokil
Lettor," for some years previous to its ceasing to be published ; Mr.
J. W. Chater was the publisher and proprietor of *Chater's Illustrated
Annual*, containing Tyneside songs and tales, to which Mr. Horsley
often contributed ; Mr. J. W. Haggerston is the Chief Librarian of
the Public Library ; Mr. W. H. Hastings and Mr. H. Heppell were
intimately associated with Mr. Horsley in connection with Reid's Railway Guide ; and Messrs. Thomas and George Allan are the Booksellers,
of Blackett Street, and were the publishers of several of Mr. Horsley's
Tyneside songs in leaflet form.

A PLEA FOR THE AGED FEMALE SOCIETY.

Oh! sad pathetic words to hear!
   An aged female she has grown ;
For her life now is in the " sere
   And yellow leaf," when youth has flown.
She once was young, she once was dear ;
Now, life for her is in the " sere."

There was a time when she was fair,
   With sparkling eyes and laughing face,
When from her brow her glossy hair
   She braided back with childish grace.
She then was young, she then was dear ;
Now, life for her is in the " sere."

Her girlish form, once lithe and neat,
   With shapely limbs and rounded arms,
Now stoops, and age and lagging feet
   Show but the grave of youthful charms.
She then was young, she then was dear ;
Now, life for her is in the " sere."

Yes, she is old and weak and worn,
   And feebly treads life's weary way ;
Of hope bereft, of beauty shorn,
   She still must wait life's closing day.
She once was young, she once was dear ;
Now, life for her is in the "sere."

Can hearts that beat and still are true
   Refuse the succour that might save,
And not be moved somewhat to do
   To smooth her path towards the grave ?
She once was young, she once was fair ;
But now her wants should be our care.

October 26, 1885.

THE DOVE OF PEACE!

O, dove! as from the ark thou sped away
And gazed upon our world, to floods a prey,
Say, didst thou see beneath thy lofty scan
Aught of the lifeless wreck of deluged man?
To thee, it was ordained, as Scripture saith,
To look upon our nature's first great death.
As to and fro' thou went, and found no root,
Nor twig, nor branch, on which to set thy foot,
What was the scene that met thy wondering eyes
Beyond the waste of waters and the skies?
Sawest thou that Holy Spirit which did move
The primal waters, in his work of love,
When earth, and sea, and sun, and moon, obeyed
His mighty mandate, and a world was made?
Or heardest thou of promise made to man
In Eden's garden, when the curse began,
That though "the serpent with its subtle tread
Should bruise his heel, yet He should crush its head?"
Sawest thou, those beams of mercy sent
Across God's arc, in holy covenant;
"That while the earth remains there should not cease
Of day and night, of seedtime and increase?"
Or didst thou see that bright and guiding star
That led the Eastern Magi from afar
To seek in Bethlehem that fount of love—
Good-will and peace to man, thou heavenly dove?
For unto us, on that great birthday morn,
"A son was given," yea, "Christ the Lord" was born!
But it might not be thine to see or know
Of One whom all the past was meant to show;
Thou couldst not know of Jesu's stripes and tears,
Of his betrayal, nor his servant's fears,
Nor of his passion, nor of Calvary's cross,
Whereon he suffered, to the grave's great loss;
Of victory over man, and death its sting,
That conquering both, he light and life might bring!
Return thee now unto thy ark of rest,
And leave me here on mine—a Saviour's breast.

THE CHRISTIAN'S DAWN.

SUGGESTED BY J. R. WALLER'S "THE COMING DAWN."

Ah ! Poet of this world how weak the food
That thou would'st give to feed my love of good.
As in the parable, to Christians known,
I ask for bread, thou givest me a stone!
The landmarks that my feeble footsteps guide
Thou would'st remove, my faith thou dost deride.
My humble prayer, my simple guileless creed
Offend thee, though they are my strength in need.
They are not born of science it is true,
But then they keep in me life's end in view.
Is there no " dogma " in thy science, brother?
Do we not change one dogma for another?
Thou speakest unto me of flowers that bloom,
But then, beneath their perfume lies the tomb,
And though their beauty charms my human eye
Unlike my soul, they only bloom to die.
Thou pointed me to learning's "bright to-morrow,"
But will its pathways keep from sin and sorrow?
Though all its myst'ries I should solve and prove
Will it within me sow one seed of love?
Thou whisperest to me of " settled strife,"
Alas! I know there is no rest in life.
Thou dost but give me vague and sounding words,
I look to One on high, the Lord of lords.
He is my strength, in Him alone I trust,
I live in faith and tread the path that's just;
I've hopes outside this life, a soul to save,
My dawning, then, must be *beyond* the grave.

THE END.

Rest troubled heart, now then be still,
   Cease beating in this weary breast,
Go lay thee 'neath yon rising hill,
   Whose winds shall soothe thee to thy rest.
One thought for friends soon to be left,
   One thought for them who've gone before,
One sigh for them to be bereft,
   Then sleep that sleep which wakes no more.

TIME AND ETERNITY.

"For in His presence is the fulness of joy, and at His right hand
are pleasures for evermore."

BIRTH.   When breath came in
      Thy mortal frame
      Leaped forth to life
      And then became
  The field of flowers, of thorns, of sin.

YOUTH.   Life is so sweet,
      All seems so well,
      The path all flowers,
      No fears to quell
  Thy buoyant heart, nor stay thy feet.

AGE.   But youth is by
      And age begun ;
      Thy running sands
      Are nearly done,
  And thou must "face the wall" and die.

DEATH.   When thy last breath
      Shall from thee go,
      And life's high tide
      Shall backward flow,
  And leave thee on the shore of death,

  Then it shall be
      One feeble cry,—
      One wistful look,—
      One gasp,—one sigh,—
  The tomb ; and then—ETERNITY.

REST.   The battle's o'er,
      The victory's won !
      Youth, Age, and Death
      No more can come
  To mar thy peace on yon bright shore.

REWARD.   No eye hath seen
      No ear hath heard
      Nor heart conceived
      The great reward
  Laid up for faith which tried hath been.

FLOWER SERVICE HYMN.

O ! bless the Lord for all the sunny hours
That clothe the hills and dales with beauteous flowers,
With trees and blossoms that perfume the air,
And all that makes our earth so bright and fair.

O ! bless the Lord for every kindly heart
That through these gifts of his sweet joys impart,
They teach us lessons from both flower and field
How God's great mercy is in them revealed.

O ! bless the Lord for all life's varied powers
That yield such joys from simple fruits and flowers ;
Yea, Solomon in all his wealth and ease
Was not arrayed in garb so rich as these.

We bless Thee, Father, in thy heaven above,
And offer these our flowers—first-fruits of love ;
They, Lord, are thine, thy own we only give,
For we and they and all things in Thee live.

ON THE DEATH OF R. P. PHILIPSON,

Formerly Town Clerk of Newcastle-upon-Tyne.

Full eighty short summers have faded away—
Now Death has forbidden him longer to stay ;
The form once majestic, the eye once so clear,
Are wrapt in that sleep that awakens not here!
What the verdict may be when the record is read
We know not, nor would we speak light of the dead ;
Sincere in his friendships, tho' stern to his foes,
He cared not his innermost thoughts to disclose.
In mein unpretending, averse to the proud,
He was felt in his life, though he shrank from the crowd.
Now stilled is that force that was wont to command
Through the deep subtle mind and the vigorous hand ;
No more shall those lips their old wisdom repeat,
Nor the heart of his manhood responsively beat.
Let him sleep, as he fell, in his harness encased,
While the world from the tablet of memory's erased ;
This life's " fitful dreaming " for him is now o'er,
And its hopes and its fears shall disturb him no more.

Newcastle, December 18th, 1879.

LINES OF SYMPATHY,

ON THE DEATH OF ANDREW OCTAVIUS REID,

Aged 10 Years.

So fresh, so full of hope and joy,
　Yet called, alas ! so soon away;
His young life passed without alloy—
　He leaves his childhood's mirth and play.

But yesterday we looked upon
　His laughing face and beaming eyes—
Death's angel came ; and now he's gone
　To his new home beyond the skies.

Ah ! 'tis the will of him who gave,
　To take again his gift away ;
And 'tis his will that through the grave
　His loved ones pass to endless day.

Then let us weep and meekly bear
　The cross which Heaven to us hath sent,
Though hard to lose the young and fair—
　They are not ours, they're only lent.

Printing Court Buildings, Newcastle,
May 26th, 1884.

ON THE DEATH OF FRANK E. BELL,

Late Manager of the Theatre Royal, Newcastle.

He sleeps ! " perchance to dream ; " if so, 'tis well ;
Sleep on ! and from thy labours rest, dear Bell.
The drama of " life's fitful dream " is o'er—
Played out, to be rehearsed on earth no more !
The scene is changed. The fleeting stage of time,
With all its imag'ry and art sublime,
Thou'lt share no more ; thou hast fulfilled thy *rôle ;*
Death ends the plot, the grave becomes thy goal.

　.　　.　　.　　.　　.　　.　　.

The " silver cord is loosed, the bowl is broken,"
The dying wish expressed, the last word spoken ;—
And now, one kindly heart is stilled for ever
One form removed from sight—from mem'ry never !

Feb. 7th, 1882.

ON THE DEATH OF MISS H. HASTINGS.

The drooping flower now faded lies,
   And calmly sleeps its sleep of death,
Yet from it still there seems to rise
   The fragrance of the flowret's breath.

Fair as the lily, young as fair,
   Earth could not call her long its own ;
Her spirit, shrinking from life's care,
   To realms celestial now hath flown.

Thou, Shepherd, in thy loving arms,
   We lay this tender lamb to rest ;
The grave receives the withered charms,
   Her soul finds safety on thy breast.

Mourn not that Jesu bade her come,
   Nor tears of hopeless sorrow weep ;
Rejoice that he hath called her home,
   Hers is not death, she doth but sleep.

October 7th, 1882.

TO THE ANGEL OF DEATH.*

O ! Death, come softly to my side,
   And whisper low thy dread command ;
When I no longer here may bide,
   Then take me gently by the hand.
If thou must come, O ! then be kind,
And think of them I leave behind.

Come not in wrath nor in the storm,
   Nor in the pestilence nor war,
But rather in thy softer form
   Of gentle swoon or slumber's car.
If thou must come, O ! then be kind,
And think of them I leave behind.

* This is one of Mr. Horsley's unpublished pieces, and is full of sympathy and love for those who were dear to him. The last verse was evidently written at a later date than the preceding verses, and after they were signed and dated. It is a singular coincidence, and worthy of remark, that there was a heavy snowstorm on the day of his death, and the ground was covered with snow when he was laid in his last resting place.

Come not in treachery nor hate,
  Nor take me in some deed of sin ;
But lead me to thy pathless gate
  In love, and bid me enter in.
If thou must come, O ! then be kind,
And think of them I leave behind.

Come clothed in mercy, come in peace,
  While friends and loved ones round me mourn,
Whose voices may, as life doth cease,
  Accompany me to yonder bourne.
If thou must come, O ! then be kind,
And think of them I leave behind.

Come when the flowers are blooming fair,
  In autumn or in budding spring;
When nature's perfume fills the air,
  And birds my requiem sweetly sing.
If thou must come, O! then be kind,
And think of them I leave behind.

I fear thee, yet I seek thee, Death,
  Thy wakeless sleep a rest doth bring ;
May faith and prayer in my last breath
  Disarm thee of thy bitter sting.
If thou must come, O ! then be kind,
And think of them I leave behind.

February, 1886.

* * * * * *

O ! come not when the driven snow
  Lies thick beneath the mourners' feet,
It seems so cold to be laid low
  Beneath a wintry winding sheet.
If thou must come, O ! then be kind,
And think of them I leave behind.

LONGFELLOW.

Sweet Bard of the States, that fair land o'er the sea,
No more shall soft cadences rythm from thee ;
The silence of death stills thy eloquent tongue !
In numbers thy own be thy requiem sung.
For what can more fitly speak to us of thee
Than thy words that found birth in the land of the free ?

> " The land of song within thee lay
> Watered by living streams,
> Those lids of fancy sleep to-day
> That to the gates of Paradise
> In holy thoughts were wont to rise ;
> Now closed like angel's wings."*
>
> " From their distant flight
> Through the realms of light
> There falls into our world of night
> As the murmuring sound of rhyme."
>
> " They are the tongues
> Of the Poet's songs
> Murmuring of joy that to heaven belongs
> Entering a happier clime."†

Newcastle, March, 1882.

* " Views of the Night."   † " Birds of Passage."

ON THE DEATH OF JOHN CLAYTON,

Formerly Town Clerk of Newcastle-upon-Tyne.

J ust as his century of circling years
O n Time's great dial was about to show
H is long and useful life, undimmed by tears,
N ow death hath garnered, and laid gently low.

C alm as a lake his pilgrimage has been,
L inking the law with antiquarian lore,
A Bruce his henchman, so to-day is seen
Y on grand memorial in Cilurnum's store.
T hough Tyne and Solway from each other fall,
O ne bond unites them—Hadrian's Roman Wall,
N ow Clayton's name the last will e'er recall.

Newcastle, July 14th, 1890.

D

IDDESLEIGH.

I n his place at the front, his honours around him,
D evoted to duty the summons hath found him,
D eath bringing release from the labours of State,
E ven plucking the sting from the arrow of Fate ;
S o falls the true statesman whose historic name
L inks the old house of Northcote with titles and fame,
E ndeared to his country, his party, his friends,
I n his death finding triumph where vict'ry oft ends ;
G oing calmly, yet bravely, to spend his last breath,
H e dies, and in harness, yet lives in his death.

January 18th, 1887.

THE DEATH OF LORD BEACONSFIELD.

A piercing rumour thrills throughout the land.
A dread calamity ! Death's icy hand
Hath chilled a heart and paralyzed a brain
Whose subtle force we ne'er shall know again.
Be still, ye envious tongues! for once let peace
Beguile you of your joy, let rancour cease ;
The lion of a tribe lies still in death,
Disturb ye not his slumbers with a breath.
Awake to consciousness ! O fools and blind !
And realise your loss ; a giant mind
Has sunk to sleep, your nation's foremost life
Lies cold in death, amid your hollow strife.
He sleeps, embalmed in every British heart
That beats for empire, and would bear its part
In keeping England's banner, once unfurled,
Respected and unstained throughout the world.

April 19th, 1881.

51

PRIMROSE DAY.—1884.

O Beaconsfield ! thou statesman wise and brave,
All thoughts are turned towards thy wreath-clad grave :
Millions of British hearts will on this day
The homage of a grateful people pay.
The memory of thy long and great career
Will to each patriotic soul be dear ;
Death cannot rob us of thy honoured name,
Nor time obscure the lustre of thy fame ;
Our empire's greatness bears throughout the earth
Its witness to thy foresight and thy worth.
Spontaneously the nation freely gives
Undying proof that still thy memory lives,
And British bosoms will with pride display
Thy floral emblem on each Primrose Day.

April 19th, 1884.

PRIMROSE DAY.—1885.

Again we hail the sacred day's return,
On which Conservatives their breasts adorn
With modest primrose, that sweet simple flower
So dear to Beaconsfield in leisure's hour.
Thy memory, O ! Statesman ! all revere,
And homage pay unto thy great career ;
Thou who in policy and in debate
Stood forth the champion of Imperial State,
Who without patronage, or wealth, or birth,
Made England's name respected o'er the earth ;
Whose foresight and whose world-acknowledged fame
Shed lustre on thy country and thy name.
With pride to-day each loyal heart will yield
Ungrudging tribute to thee, BEACONSFIELD !

April 19th, 1885.

THE POOR'S HOUSE.*

We raised a noble House upon a hill,
That men might shelter in when poor and ill ;
We gave them clothing and we gave them food,
'Twas in our hearts to do the needy good.

In vain we build, in vain lay on the rate,
In vain we try to ease a bitter fate,
For man, official man, our blessings turn
To curses, " making countless thousands mourn."

Oh, creature of the flesh ! when raised to power,
Why be so prone to " strut and fret thy hour ? "
Doth helpless poverty make thick thy skin ?
Will "Nature's touch" not make thee know thy "kin?"

Ah ! slow to succour, aye, too late to save ;
Why stand between the pauper and his grave ?
Look in thy heart, then up to heaven's high dome,
'Tis thine to make the poor man's House his home.

Blanched were the lips, but strong and red the tape
That tied the hands, and let a life escape !
How sad to die, unfriended and unknown,
But oh ! to die 'mid thousands—yet alone !

Newcastle, October 14th, 1880.

* This was a case where the police doctor was called in to see a
man who was in a weak and exhausted condition, at the Central
Police Station, Pilgrim Street, Newcastle, about one o'clock on
Saturday. The man appeared to be suffering from a slight stroke,
and orders were given for his removal to the Workhouse. Owing
to the officialism at the " house," he was not admitted till six o'clock.
No doctor was sent for until Sunday, but before he arrived the man
was dead. The doctor gave it as his opinion that if he had been
removed sooner he would doubtless have recovered.—*Vide* Daily
Papers.

ENGLISH WOMEN AND BELGIAN ROUÈS.

England! are thy daughters born so fair,
Doth nature lavish on them charms so rare,
That nations envy thee and seek thy shores
To revel in the sweets of thy boudoirs?

England! are thy sons still bold and free,
Are they still proud, do they yet boast of thee?
Is honour still with them more than a name?
Is even death not pref'rable to shame?

England! art thou a nation brave and strong?
Is it thy mission still to right the wrong?
If so, then is it English, is it just,
To see thy daughters feed the Belgians' lust?

Oh, English fathers! must your souls be stung?
Oh, English mothers! must your hearts be wrung
By tales of villany, of crime, or worse,—
That make the Belgian name a parent's curse?

Base, brutal Brussels! offspring of a State
That English strength has saved from certain fate,
Is this thy gratitude, thou hateful name,
That thou our daughters should seduce to shame?

Newcastle, September 22, 1880.

THE SAILOR'S CHILD.

A sailor sailed o'er the deep blue sea ;
A mariner kind and brave was he ;
He feared not the storm, nor the driving foam,
But his heart sank low for his child at home.

His wife lay cold in her early grave,
But her youngest child he sought to save.
He kiss'd his cheek as he said good-bye,
But saw through his tears that the child must die.

Far o'er the wide blue main was he,
No tidings could reach him upon the sea ;
But oft as his good ship ploughed the deep,
With thoughts of his child he was rocked to sleep.

Each " watch," as he rose, he looked to the sky,
He breathed forth a prayer as he gazed on high ;
Then he turned his eyes o'er the white sea foam,
And thought of his dying child at home.

The storm might rage, and the ship might toss,
But none were near him to breathe his loss :
At home, sweet cherubs on a calm spring day
Had borne the soul of his child away.

Like the lightning's gleam the news they flash ;
It meets him on shores where strange seas dash ;
In tears and with sobs, he bows his head :
" O Lord ! give me strength ; my child is dead ! "

Sandyford, April 3rd, 1882.

THE EMIGRANT'S SIGH.

They told me that my island home,
    Which until then was dear to me,
Was old, oppressed, and overgrown,
    With selfish wealth and poverty.

They pointed me to lands more fair
    That I would find across the sea,
Where I the sweets of wealth might share
    In tempting ease and liberty.

I bade farewell to home and friends,
    And this it wrung my heart to do,
But hope and youth to travel lends
    A charm that oft deceives the view.

I cross'd the rolling main with joy,
  And built gay castles in the air,
Foresaw a life without alloy,
  A happier home, a land more fair.

Alas! how rude has been the shock
  Of my awakening over here ;
No friends, alone, my little stock
  Of hard-won wealth all gone, fore'er.

I'm helpless here—an alien shore
  Knows not my voice nor cares for me;
I seek in vain, like many more,
  For work, for help, for sympathy.

Home of my birth, I turn to thee
  With longing eyes and aching breast;
Oh, that I might return and be
  Safe on thy shore, at home, at rest!

Newcastle, November, 1879.

THE RAFT ON THE OCEAN.*

I saw a raft upon the sea,
  'Twas floating to and fro ;
And why that raft just there should be
  I cared not then to know.

My life is spent upon the deep,
  My day breaks with the foam ;
The billows rock me to my sleep,
  The restless sea's my home.

The cry, " A sail appears in sight,"
  Arouses fore and aft :
But, oh, the cheek is blanchèd white,
  When we behold a raft !

* Captain Storrock reports :—On the 22nd April, the weather being fine, he observed a raft well constructed. He passed close to it. After passing the raft his attention was called to two dead bodies. His ship was under sail at the time. He did not stop; he passed the raft within sixty yards, and the bodies within thirty yards.—Captain of " Scotia's Queen's " report.

A raft! a raft! upon the main!
Ah! who can tell the woe,
The sad despair, the dying pain,
    That raft was doomed to know?

Is there no life upon its deck,
    Is there no shred to tell
The fearful storm, the hopeless wreck,
    That some good ship befell?

Is there no waif upon the sea,
    No floating lifeless form,
Which might reveal to you and me
    The story of that storm?

Are rafts a thing of every day?
    Is wreck, or death, or worse,
Too trifling when it comes our way
    To turn us from our course?

O, sailors! had you only known
    How some, of friends bereft,
With hope deferred, heart sick had grown,
    The raft you'd ne'er have left!

You would have searched it through and through,
    And made it tell its tale,
Revealing sadly all it knew
    Of that disastrous gale.

Around your course a history lay,
    Alas! by you unread;
It might have brought to us to-day
    Some message from the dead!

The Atalanta met the gale
    With noble hearts and brave;
The raft, the corpse, tell but one tale—
    A wreck, a watery grave.

Newcastle, June 14th, 1880.

THE SUNDERLAND CALAMITY.

"Rachel weeping for her children, and would not be comforted,
because they are not."– *Matt.* ii. 18.

186 CHILDREN CRUSHED TO DEATH, AT AN ENTERTAINMENT GIVEN IN THE
VICTORIA HALL, ON SATURDAY, JUNE 16TH, 1883.

A wail of deep sorrow thrills over the land,
And spreads desolation on every hand ;
Poor fathers and mothers their hearts have been wrung,
And bitter lament bursts from every tongue.

But a few short hours and children dear,
Who had left their homes, without thought of fear,
In the simple desire for childish joys,
Had gathered in hopes of the fatal toys.

A thousand poor things—little darlings all—
Were gathered within the Victoria Hall,
So happy they looked—'twas a charming sight
To behold how they chattered and laughed with delight.

But who would have thought that this sight could have been
So suddenly changed to a terrible scene ?
That those dear little forms could, almost in a breath,
Have been crushed in their smiles by a horrible death.

Onward they rushed with impatience and glee,
Nor dreamt of the holocaust soon they would be,
Alas ! on each other they pressed to the door,
And knew not they'd see their dear parents no more.

They fell on each other a terrible heap,
A mass of crush'd forms in that staircase so deep,
And frantic and struggling they fearfully cried
For father or mother, then sinking they died.

Oh, mothers of Sunderland, wail for your pets !
Rush madly to rescue with moans and regrets.
Oh, fathers, your hearts will be sore when you hear
What a death has befallen the child you love dear.

Strong arms and brave hearts soon were trying to save,
But alas! near two hundred must sleep in the grave,
And the voices of parents distracted with fears,
Cried aloud in the depth of their anguish and tears.

Oh look on the face of that dear little boy,
Or that sweet little girl, of some mother the joy,
Or that group of dear children of some one the pride,
Hand in hand they went in, now they lie side by side.

There's sorrow to-day on the banks of the Wear,
There's grief for the loss of the children so dear ;
But fathers and mothers must stifle their pain,
For they know they'll ne'er see their dear children again.

Oh, merciful Jesus ! so loving and mild,
Receive in thy bosom each dear little child.
Oh, succour the suff'ring and soothe thou their pain,
And comfort the heart of each parent again.

We thank thee, O Lord, for those children saved,
May the mem'ry of this on our hearts be engraved ;
O'er the forms of the dear ones who sleep with the dead,
Sad tear-sprinkled wreaths of sweet flowers we'll spread.

Her Majesty,* moved by a motherly love,
Did her care for the little ones lovingly prove,
And many a mother, heart-stricken with grief,
In her message found comfort and transient relief.

* Her Majesty sent repeated telegrams of sympathy from Balmoral.

ENGLAND'S TRIAL.

Those prosperous years we've known of late are past—
    They came upon us almost with a bound ;
Our nation, fame, and commerce, grew so fast,
    No limit to our bold advance was found.

The world's dominion we could almost claim,
    That boundless sphere which art and science fill ;
Our prestige everywhere a power became ;
    None equall'd us in genius, force, and skill.

But lust of wealth our craving hearts enthrall'd,
    And its twin sister—sensuous delight ;
They, temper-like, up-bore us over all,
    And flashed a world of riches on our sight.

Then Speculation reared it's hydra-head,
    By senseless Capital sustained ;
Abroad, the cormorants were freely fed ;
    At home, Industry's golden founts were drained.

Dazzled with success we easily fell,
    Self-made victims of our own deceit ;
Our would-be leaders did not dare to tell
    Of mines about to spring beneath our feet.

Inflation's bubble burst, and from our eyes
    Fell off the scales that hid from us the truth
That as a nation we had lost the prize,
    And must go back to lessons learned in youth.

Then came the crash ! and like a tottering wall
    Fell fortunes that, alas, were built on sand ;
The panic-storm swept over great and small,
    From Scotland's classic homes to Cornwall's strand.

Financial ruin, and sad moral wrecks,
    Lie round about us, over which we mourn ;
Our rising hopes a sad foreboding checks—
    In vain we woo Prosperity's return.

It has been said, and truly said, of old,
    " A house divided cannot hope to stand ; "
Then let the man, whose strength lies in his gold,
    Unite with him whose strength lies in his hand.

Labour from Capital should not divorce,
    But both should rather seek to wed
For *all* their lives ; " for better or for worse "
    By amity and mutual interest led.

True union achieved, their strength combined
    They in the ranks of brotherhood enrolled,
The cunning hand joined to the fertile mind—
    Again might British commerce rule the world.

But first let honesty and truth prevail,
In all transactions between man and man,
And as a nation let us never fail
In what is right and just to lead the van.

May Britain's toiling sons be wise in time,
And cast away Trades Union's slavish chains ;
May honest work no longer be a crime,
· But all be free, in Labour, Wealth, and Brains !

Newcastle-on-Tyne, March 19th, 1879.

ENGLAND'S MISSION :

"IMPERIUM ET LIBERTAS."

Awake to power, O England! and claim thy rightful prize,
Thou mother of coming nations, wherein thy future lies !
Assert thy noble mission, it is thine to do and dare ;
Thy sons are ever conquering fresh crowns for thee to wear!
We seek not empire only, but justice, truth, and right,
Our aim is civilization through mercy's softening might !
We hold all men as brethren, and would with friendly hand
Lead all the slaves to freedom and help the weak to stand!
If God the power hath given us, shall we his gift decline,
And shrink to fill a destiny ordained by hand divine ?
Those world-renewing virtues, which to our race belong,
Are ours to bless and brighten the paths we move along !
An ensign to the nations we, our righteous rule shall be,
Dispensing peace and commerce over continent and sea ;
The dynasties of India, with prestige high and old,
And hosts of princely warriors, with palaces of gold ;
The giant Himalayas, the Ganges' sacred stream,
With regal pomp and vastness to sate the wildest dream ;
The burning coasts of Africa, Australia's southern land,
The northern tracts of Canada—a great terrestrial band—
These all are our possessions and own our genial sway,
Where freedom always blossoms in an ever dawning day !

Newcastle-on-Tyne, Feb. 4th, 1880.

O ! ZULU.

A LAMENT :—ISANDULA—RORKE'S DRIFT—THE TUGELA.

Thou dark and gloomy Continent, whose " Dogs of War "
Have snatched away our husbands, sons, and brothers,
Mock not our hearts with hopes, that hopeless are—
Give back our loved ones to their wives and mothers !

O ! that sad last parting, never more to meet ;
Our eyes with fruitless tears are doomed to flow ;
In vain we listen for their coming feet ;
How hard the fate that doth bereave us so !

Ah ! that fatal confidence that led them on
To tempt the foe, and they so unprepared !
But this, aye this, we may rely upon—
They die in doing all that might be dared.

And as they fighting fell, so, still they lie
Unshrouded, and unburied in that land ;
No soothing voice, no loving friend, was nigh
To kiss the cheek, nor press the gory hand.

But the world's great harvest morn will come ;
And though to-day in bitter tears we sow,
Yet He will bring them, bring them every one,
And we, for sorrow, then great joy shall know ?

Newcastle, April, 1879.

QUEEN VICTORIA'S JUBILEE.

Hail ! Jubilee of Queen Victoria's reign,
To British hearts a proud, auspicious year ;
A nation's voice shall raise the glad refrain,
" God bless our noble Queen," to us so dear.

For fifty pregnant years, on England's throne,
  As maiden-Queen, as wife, as mother true,
Hath she the sceptre borne, with grace her own,
  And wielded power, through love, possessed by few.

Beloved Queen! a never-setting sun
  The wide dominions of thy empire cheers ;
Thy pure and gentle rule so well begun,
  May it be blessed, and spared to us for years !

Fair Monarch of these Isles ! our Empress-Queen !
  Imperial lustre crowns thy Jubilee ;
A host of peoples now, with joy serene,
  Exult, and own thy sway, secure and free.

WELCOME PRINCE OF WALES.

Hail ! Prince of Wales, chief of a Royal line,
And thou, fair Princess, welcome to the Tyne;
Northumbria's sturdy sons have ever been
True to your noble House and to our Queen.
We bid you welcome in our City's name,
And love and loyalty we here proclaim;
With pride exulting that you condescend
To art and commerce gracefully to lend
Your Royal presence, and we freely own
Our gratitude to you and to the throne.
Authorities and people with one voice,
On this auspicious day do all rejoice ;
A day to them of hope and high renown,
Which England's future Monarch deigns to crown.

WELCOME THE ROYAL PAIR.

Right welcome ! Prince and Princess to the Tyne :
To give you loyal greetings all combine;
With hearty plaudits from our sons of toil,
We bid you welcome to our northern soil.

The Rose of Denmark comes in Royal state
To Roman station and to Norman gate,
The Conqueror, his power reared on these walls:
You come to reign within our hearts and halls.

Pons Ælii and Novi Castria's banks
Swell out in loyal jubilance, and thanks
That ye have honoured thus our noblest son,
And visited the home of Armstrong's gun.

Right welcome, Royal guests! each bosom hails
The Prince and Princess of our regal Wales;
Northumbria's hardy sons with pride declare
Their homage to their Monarch's son and heir.

ON THE EVE OF THE OPENING OF THE PUBLIC LIBRARY.

Arise! Novocastria, by Tyne's flowing stream,
And enjoy in its fulness thy realized dream.
The battle is over, the struggle is past,
Our Library Catalogue is finished at last!
'Tis a day to be proud of, a day to rejoice
That gives to a HAGGERSTON's labours a voice,
And though 'twere proclaimed with stentorian lungs
It will now speak itself with its " thousands " of tongues.
All honour be given where honour is due—
To the Staff, one and all, for their efforts so true ;
To the Typo. whose art, and the Binder whose zeal
Gave form to a work, of its kind " Nonpareil ;"
And while we announce this with hearty good will
Let the burden of praise be to HAGGERSTON still.

September 11th, 1880.

THE BRITISH EMPIRE.

Come all ye gallant races
    Who own the British name,
Your noble country's praises
    With ringing voice proclaim!

For England, Ireland, Scotland, '
    One crown unites the three:
The glorious home and birthland
    Of all that's brave and free!

Let monarchs vaunt their forces
    Of hundred thousands strong,
Britannia's brave sea-horses
    Still plough the waves along.
        For England, Ireland, Scotland, &c.

Let nations change their rulers,
    Or kings disgrace their name,
Old England stands the truer—
    Hers is a " deathless fame!"
        For England, Ireland, Scotland, &c.

Though small may be our islands,
    Our sons are free to roam ;
On distant plains and highlands
    They've founded many a home.
        For England, Ireland, Scotland, &c.

Canadian ice-bound regions,
    Australia's far-off shore,
With India's swarthy regions—
    All these we own—and more.
        For England, Ireland, Scotland, &c.

As th' eagle on the pinion
    Looks down the world upon,
So we on our dominion—
    " The sun ne'er sets thereon."
        For England, Ireland, Scotland, &c.

No foe may long resist us :
An empire's strength we boast;
Our colonies they'd assist us
To guard our native coast.
For England, Ireland, Scotland, &c.

United we're the strongest
To thwart the tyrant's hand;
We've fought for freedom longest,
And still by freedom stand.
For England, Ireland, Scotland, &c.

We've raised a righteous banner
For Empress, Queen, unfurl'd,
We bear it, to her honour—
It flaunts before the world.
For England, Ireland, Scotland, &c.

Newcastle-upon-Tyne, December, 1879.

ELECTORS PREPARE!

The fiat has gone forth
To south, east, west, and north,
Each voter's heart to thrill ;
Now Britons all prepare,
With ringing voice declare
What is your country's will !
Let it go forth one dauntless cry,
That England's fame shall never die,
While she's the home of beauty !
Electors, then, this motto scan,
" England expects that every man
This day will do his duty."

E

Remember those whose voice
Traduced your country's choice,
    And tried to blast their name ;
Who kiss'd the despot's toe,
And praised each savage foe,
    To their own endless shame !
Let it be writ in words of gold—
England's honour shall ne'er be sold
    While she's the home of beauty !
Electors, then, this motto scan,
" England expects that every man
    This day will do his duty."

Remember also those
Who boldly faced your foes,
    And raised your country's fame ;
Who feared not despot's might,
But dared to do the right,
    And glorified your name ;
Let this be writ on every shield,
My country and Lord Beaconsfield
    For me, for home, and beauty !
Electors, then, this motto scan.
" England expects that every man
    This day will do his duty."

Britons, unite, and prove
You honour those who love
    And seek your country's weal ;
Our Islands, though they be
Mere specks upon the sea,
    An Empire's strength reveal !
Those glorious words our wish compass—
Imperium et Libertas,
    Old England's homes, and beauty !
Electors, then, this motto scan,
" England expects that every man
    This day will do his duty."

Let all the nations see
We are from Party free,
And brook no weak command ;
Although we strive for peace
Our strength we'll still increase
Nor fear invader's hand ;
Record your votes, support the men
Who saved before, and will again
Our English homes, and beauty !
Electors, then, this motto scan,
" England expects that every man
This day will do his duty."

Newcastle-on-Tyne, March 10, 1880.

AN APPEAL TO LIBERALS.

Liberals be free, free as your name implies ;
To tyrannise for Party is a Tory in disguise.
Beware, then, of coercion, no matter what the claim ;
Vote true and independent, through good and evil fame.

Liberals be just, be equal to the hour ;
Use well, but not abuse, the trust that's in your power.
Your country and your principles, be these your highest aims,
Care naught for Party shibboleths, nor interest, nor names.

Liberals weigh your action, you're forming history's page;
The world is looking on you, abjure then party rage ;
Join Liberal with Conservative, and let your verdict be,
For Empire and for Principle, with England strong and free.

MERRY CHRISTMAS.

Welcome is the merry Christmas time
With all its love and joy and peace sublime—
Its wintry heralds in the frost and snow,
Its bright-green holly and the mistletoe,
Its sweet re-unions of long-parted friends,
And all the charms that happy home-life lends.
O ! merry may it be, in cot and hall;
God give you Merry Christmas, one and all.

CHRISTMAS, THE QUEEN OF THE YEAR.

All hail ! Merry Christmas, the Queen of the year,
    That brings to each homestead some joy,
With its festive delights and abundance of cheer,
    And its happiness free from alloy.

Advance, Father Time, with rich gifts in thy hand,
    With thy holly and "mistletoe bough ;"
Send forth thy glad greetings all over the land,
    And light on each hearth a bright glow.

The city's great heart has been lulled into rest,
    And the hum of the toilers is still,
That the high and the low may together be bless'd
    In the brotherly bonds of good-will.

Tell the lonely and desolate everywhere
    That their troubles a season shall cease;
For the Queen of the year bids humanity share
    In the "Message of love and of peace."

Ring out, then, ye bells, with your mellow-toned tongues,
    And ye choristers swell the glad sound;
Give a welcome right hearty in carolling songs,
    Which the breezes shall carry around.

For the day hath returned when each heart should rejoice,
    When each board should be loaded with cheer;
When each Christian should welcome with eloquent voice
    "Merry Christmas," the Queen of the year.

THE PARTING YEAR.

Good-bye, Old Year ! we almost grieve to part,
For time hath wound thy fetters round my heart—
In many an incident of joy and pain,
Which memory often may revive again.

Good-bye, Old Friend, go join those buried years
Which like thee once were full of hopes and fears ;
Like thee, they each came marching gaily on,
Like them, thou too wilt soon be past and gone.

Good-bye ! good-bye ! comes forth from youth and age,
Thy exit ends a scene in life's great stage ;
Yet still Old Year as thou dost pass from view,
Thou dost best usher in to us the New.

Welcome, New Year ! come in, thou honoured guest,
A welcome will we give thee of the best ;
Old Father Christmas came with merry cheer
And bade us welcome in the young New Year.

December 27th, 1883.

FAREWELL, OLD YEAR !

Farewell, Old Year, with all thy string of days ;
No more on thee shall Sol reflect his rays ;
No more the placid moon, with silver beam,
Will shed her light upon thy troubled dream.

Thy weeks are gone, with all their Sabbath morns,
Whose sacred rest our toiling life adorns ;
Thy hast'ning hours, and minutes, all are done —
Have fleeted just as though they'd ne'er begun !

And yet thou art, and wilt for ever be,
Recorded in this world's great history,
As one with whom high lofty hopes were born :
As pregnant with an era's dawning morn.

Bells rang thee in, and bells will ring again
To mark thy passing, and thy ended reign ;
And as their cheerful sounds we mortals hear,
One thought for thee—then welcome the New Year.

Newcastle, Dec. 30th, 1880.

THE BIRTH OF THE YEAR.

The morning stars sang forth with joy—
A New Year's born, Time's infant boy.
Their music rang throughout the spheres,
In welcome to the hope of years.

They sang of years gone by of old,
Of morns and eves a thousandfold,
Of all the hopes and joys and fears
They'd welcomed in with hosts of years.

They sang, Old Time is ever new;
Each moment's born afresh for you.
In clouds and sunshine, smiles and tears,
'Twere well to welcome in the years.

Roll on, then, Time, with grand refrain,
The old years die to live again,
And earth unites with boundless spheres
To welcome in the bright new years.

December 31st, 1881.

EIGHTY-THREE.

The days run out like minute sands
Marked on life's page by Time's own hands ;
The once young year now old we see,
And hope beats high for Eighty-Three !

This year's great pulse will soon be o'er,
'Twill sink to rest like many more,
And life's new ledger we shall see
Marked folio one of Eighty-Three !

New governments may rise and fall,
New events forth new men may call,
Yet nought that's new more new shall be
Than New Year's Day of Eighty-Three !

December 29, 1882.

OH, COME TO THE SEA.

Oh, come now with me,
Come down to the sea,
Where the billows roll into the Tyne ;
And there you shall see
Youth happy and free,
A sporting at Neptune's shrine ;
How pleasant to play
All through the long day
At the edge of the briny shore ;
While ladies so gay
Steal the men's hearts away
Which they never intend to restore !

Oh, come then with me,
To the ever green sea,
Where the billows roll into the Tyne ;
And there you shall see
Life happy and free,
A sporting at Neptune's shrine !

How jolly to bathe,
Or breast the green wave,
In a skiff o'er the waters so free ;
While some they will lave,
Others willing and brave
Make the oars to dip into the sea !
How rakish to ride
O'er the sands by the tide,
As the breakers roll on to the beach ;
Our chargers we guide
In their galloping stride
While we strive the far goal to reach !
Oh, come then with me, &c.

How charming to bound
To the music's sweet sound,
Or to watch the swift waltzers sweep by ;
While amid the gay round
Some dear lover is found,
Whom we know by the glance of his eye ;

Oh, come then with me,
To the ever green sea,
And sport ye at Neptune's shrine ;
And there you shall see,
Life happy and free,
Where the billows roll into the Tyne.
        Oh, come then with me, &c.

Newcastle, June, 1881.

THE ONE-HORSE CAR.

Now all you gents whose hearts are kind,
A poor old horse never sit behind ;
You wouldn't be cruel—and right you are—
Then please don't ride in a one-horse car.
    A one-horse car ; a one-horse car ;
    Then please don't ride in a one-horse car.

'Tis nice to ride in the noon-day heat
In a cab, or tram, o'er the stony street ;
'Tis nice to be kind, as some folks are,
Then who would ride in a one-horse car?
    A one-horse car ; a one-horse car ;
    Then who would ride in a one-horse car?

"A Horse ! A Horse !" was the king's request ;
But a couple I'm sure would suit me best ;
And when I go out, be it near or far,
I never will ride in a one-horse car.
    A one-horse car ; a one-horse car ;
    I never will ride in a one-horse car.

Money, they say, makes the mare to go ;
But wrung from a one-horse slave, oh, no !
Then those who wouldn't our feelings jar
Wait a few minutes for the two-horse car.
    The two-horse car ; the two-horse car ;
    Wait a few minutes for the two-horse car.

MY KNIGHT NO MORE I'LL SEE.

A lady loved a Knight so gay ;
She watched him as he rode away ;
He kissed his hand, and spurred his steed,
Then dashed away with lightning speed.
   The lady sighing, cried, ah, me !
   I fear my Knight no more I'll see !

O'er many a land he wandered far ;
He fought and bled in many a war ;
To friend or foe he showed no fear,
But bore him like true cavalier.
   The lady sighing, said, ah, me !
   I fear my Knight no more I'll see.

Where'er he rode, with lance in rest,
A fearless heart beat in his breast ;
The aged and the maiden fair
None dare insult were he but there.
   The while his lady sighed, ah, me !
   I fear my Knight no more I'll see.

Oft wandered she the lonely wood ;
Oft on the battlement she stood ;
But ever at the evening hour
She longing gazed out from her bower,
   And sadly sighed, and said, ah, me !
   My gallant Knight no more I'll see.

Her father bade her braid her hair,
And wear again her smile so fair :
"Another Knight I'll bring to thee,
And he shall be a son to me."
   She sadly sighed, and said, ah, me !
   My gallant Knight no more I'll see.

A rich and noble suitor came,
And tried to light Love's tender flame.
" My name and wealth are thine," said he,
" If thou my loving bride wilt be."
   She sadly sighed, and said, ah, me !
   Sir Knight, no heart have I for thee.

But, hark! a sound strikes on her ear ;
Her heart beats quick with hope and fear ;
A prancing steed speeds o'er the plain,
And brings her back her Knight again.
No more she sighs, but sings with glee,
My gallant Knight's returned to me !

Sandyford, Newcastle.

THE FAIR-HAIRED MAID.

I dearly love the fair-haired girl,
To me she seems divine,
The witching charm of each bright curl
Enchants this heart of mine.

Her eyes are blue, of lustrous hue,
Her cheeks are rosy red ;
Her lips they have the plumpness, too,
As if on kisses fed.

Some love the dark brown tresses, aye,
Dark as the raven's wing ;
But, oh! I love them golden, yea,
As golden as this ring.

There's burning love and softness there
In every glancing shade ;
My darling blonde, my beauty rare,
My lovely fair-haired maid !

LOVE'S LOOK.

Look on me, love ! with those dear witching eyes,
Turn not away from one who loves thee well,
List to the language of my pleading sighs,
Let them declare the love I fain would tell.

Look on me, love ! my heart is as a book,
Wherein thy face reflected thou wilt see ;
'Tis printed there each time that thou dost look,
In lines that glow with burning thoughts of thee.

ST. VALENTINE'S DAY.

Come, gentle friends, and list to me,
　I will not keep you long;
Both young and old will sure agree
　With this my little song.

　　If there's a day in all the year
　　　That with a wreath I'd twine,
　　It is the happy day, my dear,
　　　Of sweet Saint Valentine!

When youth and health their sweets impart,
　And life knows no alloy,
'Tis then that love doth touch the heart
　And tap the springs of joy.
　　　· If there's a day, &c.

When wedded joys their riches give
　In pledges sweet and fair,
In them, again, our youth we live,
　And in their pleasures share!
　　　If there's a day, &c.

How bright the hope that reigns around,
　And ushers in that morn;
When in each hand and heart is found
　Some proof of love new-born!
　　　If there's a day, &c.

And still as down life's vale we go,
　And memories sweet retain,
'Tis of the dearest joy we know
　To dream of youth again!
　　　If there's a day, &c.

Newcastle-on-Tyne, February 10, 1880.

KINDNESS EVERYWHERE.*

Air—" March of the Men of Harlech."

See, a mighty host advancing,
Troops of little bright eyes glancing,
Uncle Toby's joy enhancing,
　　Sitting in his chair.
They are bands of Mercy's teachers,
Father Chirpie's little preachers,
Pledged to show to helpless creatures,
　　Kindness ev'rywhere.

　　Here's a noble mission,
　　For each young ambition,
　　Live to guard both beast and bird
　　　　From cruelty and oppression ;
　　Come and join our ranks, dear brothers,
　　Bring your children, fathers—mothers,
　　Let these words go forth with others,
　　　　Kindness ev'rywhere.

See, the great Big Book lies open,
Uncle Toby's vows unbroken,
Tens of thousands now have spoken
　　Fealty to him there.
Our D.B.S. is ever growing,
Seeds of goodness it is sowing,
And its members ever showing
　　Kindness ev'rywhere.

For mercy we're contending,
All helpless things defending,
Resolved to stand, a faithful band,
　　Our noble cause extending.
Uncle Toby's banner o'er us,
Cruelty shall flee before us,
While we raise the loving chorus,
　　Kindness ev'rywhere.

* This was one of the Prize Songs composed to celebrate the enrolment of 100,000 members of Uncle Toby's Dicky Bird Society, and sung at the great demonstration in the Tyne Theatre, Newcastle, July 5th, 1886.

THE BICYCLE BELL.*

It's ho ! to be off on the road, my boys,
  With a bright and a breezy sky ;
To be mounted is one of the wheelman's joys,
  On his bicycle fleet and high.
With bearings well oil'd, and pedals made taut,
  And spider wheels bright and clean,
With his lamp, tools, and satchel he cares for nought
  As he rides on his roadster machine.
For there's never a sound he loves so well
As the cheery clink of the bicycle bell.

It's ho ! for the meet on a glorious day,
  . When the season is fairly in,
With the captain ahead, as he leads the way
  For twenty good miles at a spin ;
As they rattle along at a lightning speed,
  And pass everything on the road—
Say who is not proud of his iron steed
  As it cleverly carries its load.
For there's never a sound we love so well
As the cheery clink of the bicycle bell.

Then see how they marshal in Indian file,
  How smartly each saddle they fill ;
How swiftly they cover each good level mile,
  And gallantly bend to the hill. ·
A glow of real pleasure each rider must feel,
  As he merrily joins in the song ;
We know of no life like a life on the wheel,
  As we treadle the roadster along.
For there's never a sound we love so well
As the cherry clink of the bicycle bell.

* This spirited and exhilarating song was written for and
appeared in the Christmas Number of *The Cyclist*, for 1882. It was set
to music by Mr. Thomas Bell, of Newcastle. Both words and music
have a merry ring about them, calculated to fill the heart of the
cyclist with joy either when on the road or at the festive gathering.

TOASTING STANZA.

Here's success to each cycling club, my boys ;
  Here's a health to each captain as well ;
And a health to each friend, who a pleasure enjoys,
  In the clink of the bicycle bell.
May pluck and good fellowship ever prevail :
  May the season prove happy and long ;
May we always give comrades a hearty all hail !
  And be welcomed with toast and with song.
For there's never a sound we love so well
As the cheery clink of the bicycle bell.

THE TEA KETTLE'S SONG

I sat by the fire and silently gazed
In the bright ruddy embers that cheerily blazed ;
The kettle sang sweetly a homely refrain,
Which I often remember with pleasure again.

It sang of the time when I sat as a bride
Enclasp'd in his arms at my own fireside,
When thankfully trusting in heaven above,
He called me dear wife in sweet accents of love.

It sang of the time when my first little child,
As it lay on my knee, looked towards it and smiled,
While I sang in a lullaby father's dear name,
Which I ever repeated till homeward he came.

And still it keeps singing with spluttering glee
As time brings back children and husband to me,
And the days even now seem more happy and long
As I listen with joy to the Tea Kettle's Song.

THE MAY-DAY HORSE SHOW.

Gee up, my boys ! heck, har, gee wo ;
See the horses march in the May-Day Show.
With harness bright and prancing head,
Each steed steps out with a stately tread.
    Gee up, my boys ! heck, har, gee wo !
    See the horses march at the May-Day Show.

Join, masters, with a right good will ;
Join, drivers, too, and show your skill ;
Dress up your trappings with ribbons gay,
There's a prize to win on the First of May.
    Gee up, my boys ! heck, har, gee wo !
    See the horses march at the May-Day Show.

Come on, North-Eastern, with your greys,
And Carver and Hindhaugh bring your bays.
Come, Oubridge, and head the cavalcade ;
Come the smartest teams of any trade.
    Come on, my boys ! heck, har, gee wo !
    See the horses march at the May-Day Show.

For every prize proves this at least—
That the winner's smart and kind to his beast ;
And master and man should in this excel—
To be kind to their horses, and use them well.
    Come, then, my boys ! heck, har, gee wo !
    Take a pride in your nags at the May-Day Show.

Hurrah ! for the men who led the way,
For our noble show so grand and gay ;
With a hearty cheer for the Baroness,
Whose presence makes it a success.
    Come on, my boys ! heck, har, gee wo !
    A cheer for each prize and the May-Day Show.

THE TEMPERANCE FESTIVAL

ON NEWCASTLE TOWN MOOR, JUNE 28TH AND 29TH, 1882.

Come on in your thousands, come on, to the Moor,
There'll be pastime and pleasure for rich and for poor;
The cause of true temperance triumphs to-day,
And the reign of the drunkard is passing away.

The Blue Ribbon Army, a conquering band,
Has raised its fair banner throughout the whole land,
It bids you to pleasures both lasting and pure
On the wide breezy slopes of Newcastle Town Moor.

The boundless resources of knowledge and wealth
Are united to furnish enjoyment and health;
Willing hands and kind hearts are combined with a will
To reward noble effort, endurance, and skill.

Ye valleys and villages circling the Tyne,
Send forth your contingents from factory and mine;
The old and the young, and the weak and the strong,
Are welcome to join with this jubilant throng.

Come on, then, ye toilers take holiday rest,
And join in the sports and the friendly contest;
There'll be leaping, and skipping, and music, and song,
And the laughter and fun which to numbers belong.

Come forth, like young steeds, take your stand in the race
Where alone friendly rivalry finds any place;
No gambling nor discord shall trouble you here;
Happy hearts, joyful faces, your presence shall cheer.

For the forces of temperance, peace and goodwill,
Every true loving heart shall with happiness fill;
And the breezes of heaven both mellow and pure,
And sunshine, may bless the first Feté on the Moor.

Lead on, then, friends Stephens and Lambert, lead on!
And Barkas and Herdman, and you Richardson,
And Leighton and Brentnall, your guidance we need;
There's an army of thousands to follow your lead.

OH, HAVE YOU GOT A MATCH?

There's lots of things, while moving round,
   I notice every day ;
Among the rest I'm always bound
   To hear what people say.
And as the voices float along,
   Their words I often catch ;
They rise above the busy throng,
   " Oh, have you got a match?"

You'll often see the tiny kids,
   In every busy place,
Hold out their lights with open lids,
   And look you in the face ;
Though clad in rags on every limb,
   And every rag a patch,
The question comes from even him,
   "Oh, have you got a match? "

And even noisy paper boys,
   The artful little blokes,
Will hanker after manly joys,
   And sport their penny smokes ;
And if they cannot get a light,
   Their shaggy heads they'll scratch,
And ask with cunning eye so bright,
   ' Oh, have yot got a match? "

If I should take Maria Jane
   To concert or to park,
We're always making home again
   A little after dark ;
And as a tender parting kiss
   In haste I try to snatch,
Some snob is sure to spoil my bliss
   With, " Have you got a match?"

It doesn't matter where you go,
    Or what you want to do,
To fancy ball or flower show,
    Its all the same to you ;
Some lively cove, with pleasant grin,
    Will at your elbow catch—
"Excuse me, Mr. What's-your-name,
    Oh, have you got a match?"

I've no objection to the weed,
    Nor even to a smoke ;
I'd give a quid, I would indeed,
    To any civil bloke ;
But when I do the heavy swell,
    I must be on the watch,
And quite expect to hear the yell,
    "Oh, have you got a match?"

THAT BLESSED CORPORATION.

TUNE.—"Obadiah."

This noble town of ours
Is beneath some local powers
Which for folly and extravagance is rare ;
    It's always in a muddle
    Or some very dirty puddle,
Which to meddle with nobody else would care.

CHORUS—For that blessed Corporation
            Near Newcastle Central Station,
        It is always taking up some silly fad ;
            With the rent roll of a nation,
            'Tis in endless botheration,
        And is always doing something very bad.

Their servants cannot please them,
They committee and they tease them,
And with everything they do they interfere ;
It is Fowler ! Fulton ! Curry !
Come and do this in a hurry,
Then they put the blame upon their Engineer.
   For that blessed Corporation, &c.

There's a stupid Watch Committee,
Which on Bobbies has no pity,
And can boast a very clever Fire Brigade ;
Let a man be e'er so handy,
If he tastes a little brandy,
That's the very man they'll punish and degrade.
   For that blessed Corporation, &c.

No doubt with Captain Nichol
They are often in a pickle,
With the tradesmen for obstruction and the noise ;
But though blusterers they're fickle,
And retreat in such a stickle,
When they've threatened little girls and little boys.
   For that blessed Corporation, &c.

They're first in any movement
Of Fish Market-like improvement,
But the last in showing light where things are dark ;
They go pottering and dreaming,
While they let the silly Freemen
Drive the races from the Moor to Gosforth Park.
   For that blessed Corporation, &c.

They're blind to petty plund'ring,
But hold diplomas for blund'ring,
And they'll spend some eighty thousands on a *lane*,
And though the poor ratepayers
Utter for them lots of *prayers*,
Yet they'll still go metal milestone-ing *again*.
   For that blessed Corporation, &c.

They're wise on stars and gases,
But their bray betrays they're asses,
And they hide their sins beneath committee chairs,
Yet each one will remember
His good deeds at November,
When they're skirmishing for Aldermen or Mayors.
For that blessed Corporation, &c.

'Twould be a clever riddance
For to empty them like middens,
Then to cart them to the river into keels ;
Then get a Tyne steam-hopper,
Tell the man he's not to stop her
Till they're fairly out beyond the bar at Shields.
For that blessed Corporation, &c.

TRAM ! TRAM ! TRAM !

A cry was raised, " Oh ! give us trams
To ride us through the town ! "
The prayer was heard; contractors came,
And *softly* laid them down.

And still another cry was raised—
" Our trams sink under ground ! "
" We'll put them right, then," Fowler said,
" For nineteen hundred pound ! "

They paved, and rammed, and rammed, and paved,
And paved and rammed again,
But neither money nor credit was saved
By bungling committee men.

Then Simpson lots of letters read,
  And Fowler many more;
Each blamed the other, and both Kincaid,
  But none would pay the score !

The Council met—O save the mark !
  To judge between the three;
But, after hours of twaddle and talk,
  They simply left—for tea !

O ! FOR A JOB !

O ! for a thousand a year !
  To manage the affairs of a town !
O ! for a council that's queer,
  And dosen't know when it's done brown !

O ! for a nice little job
  To lay trams in the snow and the rain !
How the rate-paying wretches will sob
  When the trams are to pay for again !

O ! for apprentices two
  With permission to pocket the fee !
O ! to be right with the few
  That can square the committees for me !

O ! for a patient old horse
  In the shape of a silly old town !
Where, though matters get constantly worse,
  It's nobody's fault but its own !

O ! for a nice hazel stick,
  With a thong at the end for to whack
Those corporate hides that are thick !
  O ! wouldn't I lay't on their back !

GEORDY'S DREAM; OR, THE SUN AND THE MEUN.*

One fine efterneun, somehow or anuther,
Aw fancied that aw was as leet as a feather,
Aw gov a jump up, me weight for to try,
And afore aw weel knew, aw was up in the sky.
　　　　Te me fal de lal, lal de lal, la.

Aw kept gannin on, for aw thowt it ne use,
Te stop on the road where there wasn't a hoose;
Aw capered alang, but aw hadn't gyen far,
Till aw spied a young chep on the top iv a star.

Aw manœuvred a bit, till beside him aw gat,
Thinks aw here's the place aw want te be at;
Says aw, "Ma young chep, aw'm a stranger up here,
De ye knaw ony place where aw'll get a sup beer?"

"Young fellow," says he, "you come up frae below,
Yor axin' that question convinces me so;
But allow me to tell ye, the people up here
Neether eat, drink, nor sleep, nor yet sell ony beer."

Aw leuk'd at the chep, and aw laft in me sleeve,
For the story he telled me aw didn't believe;
Thinks aw aw've some whisky, aw bowt for me sell,
Aw'll just see if he knaws what it is be the smell.

* This clever and characteristic local song was written about forty years ago. It was the author's maiden effort, and for twenty-five years afterwards his only attempt at song writing. It was composed one evening after going to bed, when sleep withheld its balmy influence. It was sung by the author for the first time to a few friends at a social gathering, and again in 1876 at a dinner given by Mr. Andrew Reid to the employes in connection with Printing Court Buildings, when it was set up and printed for circulation amongst the workmen of that establishment, who expressed a strong desire to have a copy of it. It may be regarded as a remarkable instance of the effect of seeing oneself in print, for it seemed to open the flood-gates of a poetic stream which has continued to flow ever since.

Aw pulls oot the cork, and aw gies him a sup,
And begox in a minnet he supped it all up!
He wasted ne time, for as sure as yor there,
He held oot his glass for a little sup mair.

Aw tyeuk one mesel', and aw gav him anuther,
And axed him if he'd ony feyther or muther;
He nodded his heed, and gav two or three winks,
And says "Aye, but neither the two on them drinks."

But the awd folks had seen the two on us spreein',
And sune they come doon to see what we were deein';
And it's weel that they come, or the whisky was deun,
For 'twas nebody else but the Sun and the Meun.

At first they were awfully stiff and polite,
But the whisky sune put all their manners to flight;
And sune they enquired "How's all doon at hyem?"
And axed for wor awn canny Mayor biv his nyem.

They axed if the Whittle Dene wettor wis still
Supplied te the folks at se much a gill;
If the pipes elwis burst when thor come a bit thaw,
And the wives weshed thor claes wiv a pailful o' snaw.

They axed efter Sandgate, and Pipergate te,
And said there was ne place like Newcassel Quay;
And promised, whenivver the weather was fine,
To come doon an' drink luck to the lads o' the Tyne.
                        Te me fal de lal, lal de lal, la.

NEWCASSEL AN' THE SNAWSTORM.

Teun: "Weel Deun Cappy."

Not lang since, Newcassel, se fond o' reform,
Wis astonished te find itsel' blocked wiv a storm;
For days an' for neets—aye, an' mornin's an' a'—
Thor wis nowt te be seen but greet shoors iv snaw.
              Poor Newcassel!
              Canny Newcassel!
Newcassel's been very nigh smothered in snaw.

So Fowler tell'd Fulton to tell Mr. Curry
Te cum, for he wanted him iv a greet hurry,
Te give him instructions some money te draw,
Te pay lots iv men te keep shullin' the snaw.
           Poor Newcassel !
           Canny Newcassel !
Newcassel's been very nigh smothered in snaw.

Sum cooncilmin thowt that they wadn't be fyeuls,
So they went an' they purchased sum picks an' sum shules
And aal the poor fellows that com i' thor way,
They sent them te Curry and tell'd them te say—
           Give us two shillins !
           Only two shillins !
Two shillins for shullin' the snaw aal away.

The Inspector, ne doot, his instructions had got,
Not te tyek ony notish iv nyen o' the lot ;
But te mind his awn ashes and middens at neets ;
So he left Muther Nature to clean oot the streets.
           Poor Newcassel !
           Canny Newcassel !
Newcassel's been very nigh smothered in snaw,

The Coonsil detarmin'd te lyuk inte mettors,
And hawl'd the officials afore aal thor bettors ;
They myed a commotion, and said " what a shyem ; "
Newcassel's disgraced—but neebody's te blyem !
           Poor Newcassel !
           Canny Newcassel !
Newcassel's disgraced—but neebody's te blyem !

So canny Newcassel, once famous for smoke,
Is noo gud for nowt but a Gyetsider's joke ;
Herculaneum wis dug oot iv ashes, we knaw,
But canny Newcassel's been howkt oot' o' snaw !
           Poor Newcassel !
           Canny Newcassel !
Newcassel's been very nigh lost in the snaw.

December, 1878.

NEWCASSEL DORT.

O my ! what a row in the Coonsil there's been,
  Wor Improovement Committee's got threshed ;
The corporate linen's not fit to be seen,
  So they've brought it all oot to be wesh'd !
    So they call'd for a meetin' and myed a report,
    And hinted Newcassel wis rottin wi' dort,
      Did this awful Committee ;
    And they hinted Newcassel wis rottin wi' dort !

They sent te the sooth for a grand engineer,—
  Thor wis neboddy here they could get,—
They started him off wiv a thoosand a yeer,
  And he's landed them thoosands in debt ;
    They pulled up the streets, and relaid them wi' dort,
    And twice laid the trams for the Engineer's sport,
      Did this awful Committee ;
    They twice laid the trams for the Engineer's sport.

They myed him the heed, but they gov him ne tail,
  But left them te de as they like ;
So he floonder'd aboot like a ship wivoot sail,
  And his subs. went aboot upon strike !
    Cum Fowler, cum Fulton, cum Curry, report
    Hoo lang will Newcassel be left in the dort,
      Through this awful Committee ?
    Hoo lang will Newcassel be left in the dort ?

The Coonsil cried " Fowler ! " " Committee " replied,
  That Fulton's the man ye should see ;
For sewerin' and pavin' he's thoroughly tried,
  And besides he hes nowt for te de !
    And fritened for fear Curry's feelin's wis hurt,
    They left him te de what he lik'd wiv his dort,
      Did this awful Committee ;
    They left him te de what he lik'd wiv his dort !

Se Fowler, an' Fulton, an' Curry an' all,
 Just did as they lik'd wi' the toon:
They drew each a cheque for a jolly good sal.,
 Then went away hyem an' sat doon,
  An' laff'd i' thor sleeve, for laffin's thor forte,
  At the cuddies that paid them se much te report,
   Te this awful Committee!
  That paid them se much for thor dort!

The Coonsillors met, thor disgust te de declare;
 The Committee wis up te the mark;
They arranged for the threesum the money te share,
 An' the toon may itsel' de the wark!
  Se they emptied thorsels on each other, in short,
  They were like the awd keel that they loaded wi' dort!
   Wis this awful Committee;
  That stunk the Exchange wi' thor keel loads o' dort!

October 31, 1879.

WON MILE FRAE NEWCASSEL.

Sum culls in Newcassel teuk't into thor heed
 Te dandyfy off the awd toon;
They cast metal milestyens and painted them reed,
 And planted them all up and doon!

If ye went te the byekhoose, or popt owor bye,
 Or strowl'd oot te settle the bile,
Ye wadn't gan far till a stob met yor eye,
 " Frae here te Newcassel won mile!"

Ne wonder a chep gov a sweer at his eyes,
 That had nivvor deceeved him afore,
And staggered, and said in a tone o' surprise,
 " Whey, aw've ony just left me awn door!"

Hes the toon teyn a walk or a wanderin' fit,
 Or is sumboddy just myekin gyem?
Aw cannit conceive, withoot movin' a bit,
 Hoo wor shifted " won mile" frae wor hyem!

Or hes the fond soapeys that rule in wor toon,
　Meykin' pairks in which dandies may play,
Written lees upon milestyens and planted them roon',
　Just te frighten poor tramps oot away ?

But what set the cuddies te put them doon there ?
　They're nowther a gate nor a stile ;
It beats comprehenshun te find oot frae where
　They've started te measure thor mile !

Or hes sum " contractors" been seekin' for jobs ;
　Did the Coonsil not like te say nay ;
And set them on meykin thor greet iron stobs,
　For which we'll hev sumthin' te pay !

Had they gien us good roads te wor workin' men's hyems
　Say te Bykor, or te the Sheelfield,
Cinder-walks and Ouseburns wad then ony be nyems,
　And a lang standin' sare wad be heel'd !

Had they teun all the munny the milestyens hev cost,
　And bowt thorsels hat-bands iv crape,
In mornin' for munny they've wasted and lost,
　And the wrangs that they've deun tiv a Snape !

CORPORRAYSHUN THUNDOR.

DEDDICATED TE THE SCAVINGIN' DEPAIRTMENT.

One neet, when soond asleep in bed,
　Aw heerd an awful rumour ;
Maw wife turns ower an trimlin' sed,
　" That surely mun be thundor !"

" Get up, maw man, an strike a leet ;
　Oh dear, it's awful freetenin ;
Ye knaw aw cannot bide the seet
　O' blue or forky leetenin ! "

Aw tried te passify her doon :—
Ses aw, " Ye'll be mistaken ; "
When, bang! there went anuthor soon'
That set us byeth a shaken !

Ses aw, " Wey, that's the roof com in ;
The chimley staak hes fallin ; "
An' what far mair increased the din—
The bairns began a squallin' !

Aw oot o' bed and owor the floor ;
Te save the bairns wis thinkin ;
When, as aw meyd towards the door,
There cam an awful stink in !

Aw guess'd at wonse! Ses aw, " Maw lass,
We've made an awful blunder ;
Aw saw the midden muck cairt pass ;
'Twis Corporrayshun thundor ! "

If ever h—ll should be let lowse,
Te tarrify us mortals,
Ne doot an awful smell an' noise
Will issue frev its portals !

But when it's dune it's dorty wark,
An frev this orth depairts, man ;
Aw hope it's sense o' things 'twill mark,
An' teyk wor midden cairts, man !

THE CORPORRAYSHUN STEYBLES !

"A horse! A horse! My kingdom for a horse!"

Ah, Richard, maw man, ye warrint a feul,
When ye cried oot " a horse " insteed iv " a bull ! "
There's uthors like ye, though, in humbler stayshun
That think mair iv a horse than they de i' thor nayshun !

Sum coonsillor cuddies iv a northern toon
That hev charge iv sum horses that waak up an doon,
Hev teyn'd in thor " lugs " (for what else mun aw say)
Five thoosand nine hundord for steybles te pay !

Oh, poor warkin man! ye're waakin' the street;
Ye've ne pleyce iv shelter, ye've nowt for te eat;
Gan te Wilson, the chairman, ye cannot de worse,
An' tell him ye're sure yor as gud as a horse!

Say ye'd gladly teyk leeve just te lie in a stall
That's te cost just a hundord—one hundord—that's all;
If he'll kindly consent, ye " for ivvor will pray "
As ye thenkfully rest 'mang the horses an hay!

Aw think that aw see ye, maw poor warkin' man,
But aw'll tell ye yor fortin, 'for ivvor ye gan;
Ye'll be tell'd they've ne poor, thor's ne bye-law at leest,
Te find shelter for Christian, but only for beast!

NEWCASSEL FEULS, PAST AN' PRISSINT!

Three hundord years ago Newcassel kept a feul;
Ne doot they fund him useful when the neets wis lang an'
    dull;
The Mayor an' jolly coonsillors wad often hev a spree,
An' join the Freemen for a lark te chaff the Trinitee.

Ne doot Newcassel then wis thowt a sonsie little toon,
Wiv all its narrow streets an' chares, an' walls an' towers
    roon',
Wi' fairs an' fights, an' pressgang rows, it niver wad be dull,
It mun hev been a royal toon, for then it kept a feul!

Aye, lang afore a Stephenson or Grainger saw the leet,
Or a dredger howk'd the river, or a tram ran on the street,
Or a Level led te Gyetside, or hydraulics loaded keels,
Or a Barkas dealt wi' sporrits, or the fishwives com wi'
    creels,
Or drapers dealt in babby toys, or ships went bi steam
    pooer,
Or pitmen lairned te "demonstrate," or bool upon the
    Moor,
Or the Schule Bord, or the Bobbies, teuk possession o'
    John Bull,
Aye, even in thor jolly days Newcassel kept a feul.

Whativver folks might think ov us three hundord years
  ago,
Wor toon turned oot sum tidy cheps, altho' they might
  be slow ;
Wor native worth wis not denied, we own'd wor sturdy
  race,
We let ne mongrel strangers shove wor awn frae pooer
  or place ;
But noo wor shoddy coonsillors an cliquey commit-tees
Hev fetched wor ancient borough doon, aye almeyst tiv
  its knees ;
They've spent ne end o' thoosan's ; for what? just ax the
  culls ;
Unlike wor wise forfeythors, they've myed thorsells the
  feuls!

THE BARGES IN 1881.

Wor gan te hev the Barges,
The Barges, the Barges ;
Wor gan te hev the Barges,
    And sail upon the Tyne!
The Toon pays a' the charges,
The charges, the charges ;
The Toon pays a' the charges,
    And fills us a' wi' wine !

The guns 'ill a' be firin',
Be firin', be firin' ;
The guns 'ill a' be firin',
    And flags 'ill hev te flee !
The bobbies, tee, they'll wire in,
They'll wire in, they'll wire in ;
The bobbies, tee, they'll wire in,
    An' help to meyk a spree !

Thor gan te ax the Coonsillors,
The Aldermen an' Boouce-illors,
An' a' the rob-the-toon-sillors,
    An' gie them pies an' beer.

Aye, Mayor an' Corporation,
An' River Tyne Commission,
The Market wi' ne fish in—
    The keeper 'ill be there.
The " Chamber " tee, an' Freemen,
The noisy fishwives tee, men,
An' swells frev off the Quay, men,
    Thor a' gan te be there.

An' Tinmuth, Sheels, an' Jarrow,
An' Blaydon's fire brick barrow,
An' ivvory Tyneside marrow,
    The fun 'ill hev te share,
An' Gyetside's crew tea-toatle,
Lang pipes an' baccy dottle,
Botanic beer an' bottle,
    An' the Monkeys 'ill be there !

And Chinee Johnny he'll be there,
Wiv lang pig-tail iv pletted hair,
By gum wor style 'ill myck him stare
    At us cheps on the Tyne.
An' then te wind up a' wi' grace,
Wor gan te hev a cuddy race,
An' cheps in pokes te hev a chase,
    An' myek wor Barges shine.

Noo all ye lads that can get
Frev Pipergate an' Sandgate,
Mind ye obey the maandate,
    An' all yor lasses bring !
An' ivvory Tom an' Jerry, O,
An' ivvory keel an' whurry, O,
Wiv sweethearts gay an' murry, O,
    An' mind ye'll hev te sing—

" It's weel may the keel row,
The keel row, the keel row ;
It's weel may the keel row,
    That maw laddie's in ! "

NEWCASSEL'S BRAN NEW BISHOP.*

Teun: "The Fiery Clock Fyece."

Cum, Sandgate lasses, cum up the Quay,
An' keelmen an' porter-pokemen tee,
Yor toon hes been myed a city, ye see;
    An' Newcassel hes getten a Bishop!
A greet big papor in Lundon toon
Hes collar'd the news an' wired it doon,
An' the lads an' lasses is shootin't a' roon',
    " Newcassel hes getten a Bishop!"

    Se Sandgate lasses cum up the Quay,
    An' keelmen an' porter-pokemen tee,
    Yor toon hes been made a city, ye see,
    Newcassel hes getten a Bishop!

A Quaker friend, an' a gud un aw'm sure,
Hes myed him a prissint o' Benwell Toor,
An' the ladies 'll furnish't if he's ower poor,
    For Newcassel mun hev a nice Bishop!
They've gethered sum brass biv a general sub',
For Bishops, like uthers, stand need o' thor grub,
An' he mun be a strang un hus sinners te snub,
    Mun canny Newcassel's new Bishop.

        Se Sandgate lasses, &c.

Wor awd Sint Nicklas thor gan te prepare,
An' the Mayor an' the Coonsil 'ill hev te be there,
An' mebbies they'll give him a carridge-an'-pair,
    Te mense wor Newcassel's new Bishop!

* The Rev. Ernest Wilberforce, Canon of Winchester, was the
first Bishop of Newcastle-on-Tyne.

The clark o' the toon in his garments o' silk,
I'll demand fra the Freemen a coo for his milk,
An' he'll sit wi' the " Lords " 'spite o' Cowen an' Dilke,
    For he's canny Newcassel's new Bishop.
        Se Sandgate lasses, &c.

He'll stop Sunday fairs on the Quay, that he will,
An' Davis an' Jones 'ill forsake the Sandhill,
An' the bars an' botanics ne liqors 'ill fill—
    For they'll all want te hear the new Bishop.
He'll stop the trams runnin' on Sundays as weel,
On the river ye'll nowther see steamboat nor keel,
Not a sowl i' the toon 'ill dar gammel or steal,
    For fear o' Newcassel's new Bishop.
        Se Sandgate lasses, &c.

The sowlgers an' rifles 'ill mairch te the church,
An' swagger aboot wi' thor swords i' the porch,
An' the Bobbies, oh whey, we'll leeve them i' the lurch,
    For they shannet " run in " wor new Bishop.
The Hallelu Lasses wi' thor trumpets an' drums
Needn't rouse up the folks i' the streets an' back slums
Nor the schulebord man chase the poor laddies, by gums,
    For we all noo belang tiv a Bishop.
        Se Sandgate lasses, &c.

Noo mebbies he'll pray for us sinners, whe knaws?
Aw war'nt he'll gan in for the " teetotal " cawse,
We'll all turn se gud that we'll need ne " bye-laws "
    Nor ne jails, when we've getten a Bishop.
Hurray! for Newcassel, that city se fine,
That's getten a Bishop te honor the Tyne,
Sum day he'll be axin us all up te dine,
    Then we'll drink the gud health o' the Bishop.
        Se Sandgate lasses, &c.

G

THE NEW CITY CRAZE.

Teun: "Canny Newcassel."

My eye ! what a fuss i' the toon thor's been myed—
 If thor hessen't noo, wey it's a pity ;
The high an' the low myest iv ivery trade,
 Myeks oot thor the heed o' the City !
They are not content wi' the awd fashin'd way,
 But each won mun try te be witty ;
An' becawse a new Bishop is comin' te pray,
 It's smash man ! but noo wor a City !

Thor's hardly a street where thor's owt for te sell
 But some one pretends te be funny ;
An' tries hoo the biggest o' lees he can tell,
 Te jostle ye oot o' yor munny !
He says he's a Mart or an Em-po-ri-um,
 Or sum other nyem just as pritty ;
But the latest an' fondest conceit is, by gum !
 Te be the greet shop o' the City !

If he deals in cheap slippers, or cobbles a shoe,
 Or mends folks's beuts wi' belt-leather,
Or clags on the uppers wi' blackin' an' glue,
 He sweers that thor proof agyen weather !
He print a few bills an' he hands them aroon',
 An' mebbies he pens a bit ditty ;
Declarin' tiv all byeth in country an' toon,
 He's the cobbler-boss o' the City !

If he deals in cam-pencils or copies for scheuls,
 An' slates, beuks, an' reed an' white blottin' ;
He says he's the shop that supplies City culls,
 Where feuls-cap can elways be gotten !
Or if he sells physic, as mebbies he dis,
 In bottles wiv labels the trimmist,
His pills an' fruit-salt are the regular phiz,
 For he says he's the new City Chymist !

It dissint much mettor what trade may be deun,
  Dublin stoot, London gin, or cheep " Mackey,"
He'll lug in the " City" as sure as a gun—
  City Vaults, City Pipes, and Shag 'Baccy !
Aw waddint care much iv beginnin' mesel,
  And gie'n the syem nyem te wor Kittic;
An' if yor but gam te stand two quairts o' yel,
  Aw'll call her the " Queen iv the City ! "

City Clothier, or Clogger, or City Bazaar
  Where all kinds o' nick-nacks they deal in,
Frev a bottle o' scent tiv a happ'orth o' tar,
  At prices that's far warse nor stealin'.
But then, d'ye see, they mun a' de the "grand"
  An' dress up the windows se pritty ;
So they buy up cheap guds just te suit the demand
  An' call them the best i' the City.

The way thor gan on with this grand city spree,
  Myekin' citizenship quite a hobby ;
The next thing, thor'll be City wesherwives te—
  City prig, an' a real city bobby !
An' that isn't all, but in spite o' the Mayor,
  Wor Coonsil may call a Committee
Te myek a bye-law for the lads te declare—
  " Wor the newspaper boys o' the City ! "

THE FESTIVAL ON THE TOON MOOR.

TƵUN: "Weel Deun Cappy."

Wor awd fashion'd toon hes t'yun'd intiv its heed,
That for hoppins an' races we hev ne mair need,
That babby-toy play is the best for the poor,
So they've plann'd a greet Festival on the Toon Moor,
  Hes this toon o' Newcassel, this " Canny Newcassel,"
  This Borough an' County an' City se fine.

They've formed a committee an' laid oot the grund,
An' raised i' subscriptions a h'yel thoosand pund,
They've m'yed lots o' prizes for sports an' for gam's,
An' driven folks mad wi' thor Penny Programmes,
  Hes this toon o' Newcassel, &c.

When the races should be, if the rain dissent poor,
Thor'll be seek a grand seet on Newcassel Toon Moor,
The Shoriff an' Mace, an' Toon Counsil an' Mayor,
An' all the greet folks o' Tyneside 'ill be there,
           At this toon o' Newcassel, &c.

The Freemen, gud fellows, let's gie them thor dues,
Hes gi'en us permission te join wi' the coos;
An' the sportsmen at Gosforth—'twill be a nice lark,
When we change the race-coorse tiv a teetotal park,
           At this toon o' Newcassel, &c.

Amang the greet swells that hes promised te cum,
Is Charlton, o' Gyetside, an' Dodds his awd chum;
An' mebbies freend Barkas 'ill send te the skies,
An' fetch doon a comet te win the first prize,
           At this toon o' Newcassel, &c.

Thor'll be lots o' platforms an' tents an' marquees,
An' stalls for refreshments, ice-creams, an' Game's teas;
While sum 'ill m'yek speeches, blaw trumpets an' sing,
An' uthors play "skippy" an' "kiss-in-the-ring,"
           At this toon o' Newcassel, &c.

They're gan te hev bicycles spinnin' aroond,
An' races (Oh, fie!) on a teetotal grund,
An' "hop-skip-an'-jump," aye, an' "tuggey at war,"
An' kites fleein' high, for te reach the north star,
           At this toon o' Newcassel, &c.

They're gan te hev contests wi' sowlgers an' swords,
An' "tongue-fights" te se we can say the m'yest words
An' mairchin' an' jumpin', 'cross hurdles an' backs,
An' runnin' on three legs, an' tied up in sacks,
           At this toon o' Newcassel, &c.

Thor'll be plissure for all, b'yeth the young an' the awd,
But the poor dispised publican's left in the cawd;
For the Blue-ribbon army, ye may all be sure,
'Ill stand nowt but cawd tea on Newcassel Toon Moor.
    This town o' Newcassel, this "Canny Newcassel."
    This Borough an' County an' City se fine.

THAT WRETCHED SCHULE BORD.

Noo all ye bairns o' Gyetside
Prepare yorsels for squalls,
Them goblins o' the Schule Bord
Thor doon upon yor pals.

They've raised the rate te tenpence,
Altho' the times are dull;
But they say thor's thoosands on ye
Thit's nivvor fund at schule!

They've gien thor men instrucshons
Te seek each blissed kid
Thit despises Schule Bord lairnin',
An' fine them half-a-quid.

This "liboral" Bord at Gyetside
Ageyn the poor mun strike,
An' rob them iv thor liberty
To choose the schule they like.

If ye'd all the brass that's wasted
On fancy schules and Bords,
Ne farther gyen than Gyetside,
Ye'd all be rich as lords.

Wor feythers had ne Schule Bords,
And if they scairce cud read,
They knew the way te wark at least,
And win thor daily breed!

What sowl can like a Schule Bord
That fines poor strugglin' wives,
An' myeks the bairnes' lairnin'
The misery iv thor lives?

June, 1879.

THE BAIRNS AN' THE SCHULE BORD.

" O muther, will ye let me bide
    At hyem frae schule wi' ye the day;
Thor's sumthing catches in me side:
    Aw cannit lairn, aw cannit play?

The schule is lairge and often cawd,
    The bairns are kind, but rough wi' me,
Aw think aw mun be tyekin' bad;
    O muther, let me bide wi' ye ?

Me claes is thin, an' that last storm
    Wet through me or aw gat half way;
Aw felt a' shiverin' on the form,
    Aw niver warmed at all that day."

" Maw bonny pet, maw canny bairn,
    It grieves me much to say thee No;
But aw mun work tha breed te airn
    And help te pay the rent we owe.

Tha hands is het, ma canny jewel;
    Tha fyece lyuks pinched an' wan;
Yit, tho thou mebbies thinks me cruel,
    Aw doot, maw pet, thou'll hev te gan.

Thou knaws when last thou stay'd at hyem,
    When aw wis racked wi' toothache sair,
The Schule Board tyuk the muther's nyem,
    An' fined her wiv a dozen mair."

 * . * * * * *

The mother sad to labour went,
    The ailing child to school:
Are Boards of Education sent
    The very poor so harsh to rule ?

Ye magistrates, in judgment's hour,
    Let Mercy in your hearts preside;
Restrain officious School Board power,
    And O, defend the weaker side !

AW WISH THE GUD TIMES WAD CUM.

A Topical Sang for the Times.

Teun: "The Low-Backed Car."

Noo times hev been se bad ye knaw,
  An' trade's been varry dull ;
An' wark's been scairsh an' wages sma',
  An' the bums hes had the pull ;
But noo aw hope thor better a bit,
  Folks disen't leuck quite se glum,
So aw'll leet up me pipe an' doon aw'll sit,
  An' sing o' the gud times te cum,
    Oh aw wish the gud times wad cum,
      Aw wish the gud times wad cum,
      Aw'm tired o' waitin' te see them begin,
    Oh aw wish the gud times wad cum.

Thor's monny a time for want o' wark,
  An' becawse aw had nowt te de ;
Aw've loong'd in the libr'y or the park,
  Or slaister'd alang the quay ;
Noo, leuckin' at flooers is all vary fine,
  So is watchin' the ships, d'ye see,
But an empty stomack an' nivver a coin
  Disen't help te myek much ov a spree.
    Oh aw wish the gud times wad cum, &c.

When trade wis brisk aw had ne fear,
  But spree'd me brass away
On plishur an' sport, an' baccy an' beer,
  Nor thowt ov a rainy day.
Me wife's had te pawn me Sunday claes,
  Me watch followed "up the spoot"
An' if thor's not wark in a varry few days,
  Thor's a chance they'll nivver cum oot,
    Oh aw wish the gud times wad cum, &c.

Wor folks hes often been on te me
　The temperance pledge te try,
Aw wad if aw cud, but aw cannot ye see,
　For aw elways feel see dry;
But aw think aw might join the " Army" cawse.
　For aw'm sure aw cud play the drum,
An' if clatter an' noise wad increase wor joys,
　It might help the gud times te cum.
　　　　Oh aw wish the gud times wad cum, &c.

Sumtimes aw've joined a racin' sweep,
　Or gyen an' back'd a horse,
But aw fund me brass aw had better keep,
　For me luck got elways worse ;
It myed ne matter which way aw lay'd,
　Hoo aw hedged or stud te win,
'Twas a " moral" for me the tipster said,
　'Twas a moral aw got let in.
　　　　Oh aw wish the gud times wad cum, &c.

All kinds o' trades are ower dune,
　Thor's far ower monny hands;
We'll hev te gan te the poor-hoose sune,
　Or migrate te foreign lands ;
They divvent want onny sailors noo,
　They winnet employ wor tars,
Nor de they want pitmen or bobbies in blue,
　An' thor's nowt dein' in the lang bars.
　　　　Oh aw wish the gud times wad cum, &c.

For want o' wark an' solid grub,
　An' fastin' ivvory day,
Aw soond just like a hollow tub,
　Aw'm waistin' all away ;
Once Laws did me maw photygraff,
　When aw went back agyen
He started an' yell'd oot wiv a laff,
　" Yor nowt but skin an' byen."
　　　　Oh aw wish the gud times wad cum, &c.

Wor competishun's a famous thing,
  When greet big profits is made;
It keeps doon prices an' helps te bring
  New life an' sowl inte trade:
But mind a monopoly's just the syem,
  Whether dune bi one or bi scores;
Tyek care ye aren't just changin' the nyem
  When yor capital's christen'd the " Stores."
        Oh aw wish the gud times wad cum, &c.

They taalk ov givin' poor men the land,
  " Proprietors of the soil:"
But when in the fields aw've tried me hand,
  Aw've fund it was hardish toil.
Nee doot if farmin' was myed te pay,
  It's a trade aw mebbie might choose;
But mind aw'd expect ye te set us away
  Wi' three acres an' two or three coos.
        Oh aw wish the gud times wad cum, &c.

By gum! when wark sets in agyen,
  An' aw hev a reg'lar job,
Aw'll save up me brass an' aw'll wire-in,
  An' aw'll stick tiv ivvory bob.
Wi' hungry strikes an' distress funds
  Aw'll nivver hev mair te de;
For a shillin' a day ov " test yard " pay
  Isn't quite gud eneugh for me.
        Oh aw wish the gud times wad cum, &c.

Oh divvent aw wish the time wad cum,
  When aw need te wark ne mair;
When aw'd manidg'd te save a canny bit sum,
  An' was free fre' toil an' care:
Aw think aw wad join them high-toon swells,
  That's retired an' myed thor "pile;"
That plays at the bools an' enjoys thorsels,
  In a jolly-weel-off-ish style.
        Oh aw wish the gud times wad cum, &c.

Noo Exhibitions are all the go,
 Wi' sum fine soondin' nyem;
An' thoosans mun rush te see the show,
 Nee matter hoo far fra' hyem.
But sune Newcassel 'ill hev its turn,
 Next year sic a seet ye'll see,
As nivver wes seen since we war born,
 At wor Queen's Grand Jubilee.
  Oh aw wish the gud times wad cum,
   Aw wish the gud times wad cum;
  For aw'm tired o' waitin' te see them begin,
   Oh aw wish the gud times wad cum.

OH, DINNET STRIKE.

Oh dinnet strike, me canny lads,
 Oh dinnet strike whate'er ye de,
We' wages low, an' trade se bad,
 Te strike is suicide for ye.
It isn't always what one airns,
 It's how it's spent that myeks the hyem;
For thrifty wives an' canny bairns
 Stick te yor wark, remember them.

Prosperity's a kittle slut
 That's easy huff'd an' flees away;
The wealth that years of toil hev got
 May disappear, aye, in a day.
Remember ye hev foes about,
 Whe's march 'ill not be easy stay'd,
Like vultures noo thor on the road
 Te see the funeral ov yor trade.

Then dinnet strike, me canny lads,
 Tyek common sense noo for yor guide,
Let gaffers try thor silly fads,
 The " boss " his hobby-horse mun ride.
But ye mun play a waitin' game,
 Nor fear a course of onny length,
For British skill is knawn te fame,
 An' British pluck hes wind an' strength.

TYEK MAW ADVICE, MAW CANNY LAD.

Noo canny folks byeth far an' near,
  Cum, listen what aw've got te say;
We're gettin' through anuther year,
  Anuther stage on life's rough way.
Sum's ony young, sum's gettin' aad,
  Sum's leuckin' for greet length o' days;
If onny's said or dune owt bad,
  Tyek maw advice an' mend yor ways.
      Tyek maw advice, maw canny lad,
      Tyek maw advice an' mend yor ways.

Thor's lots o' ways for one te live,
  There's lots o' gud that might be dune;
Sum like te get, sum like te give,
  But aal ye like may leeve ye sune.
So ye that's yung shud try yor best,
  Te myek the most o' youth's bright days;
For change may cum an' fairly test
  The gud or bad ov aal yor ways.
      Tyek maw advice, maw canny lad,
      Tyek maw advice an' mend yor ways.

Ambition's useful in degree,
  But pride myest elways hes a fall;
Them that lives lang will think like me,
  A humble mind's the best for all;
For upstarts fill'd wi' vain conceit,
  May flourish whiles there's sunny days;
But simple worth is bad te beat,
  And honesty's the thing that pays.
      Tyek maw advice, maw canny lad,
      Tyek maw advice an' mend yor ways.

When cheps are young they're apt te craw,
  And cocky-like ye'll hear them sing:
" Oh, sic a clivvor chep am aw,
  Aal others aw can fairly ding."

But braggin's but an empty blaw,
   The wise man's careful what he says;
An' if true wisdom ye wad knaw,
   Ye'll haud your tounge an' mend yor ways.
     Tyek maw advice, maw canny lad,
     Tyek maw advice an' mend yor ways.

If lads an' lasses only knew,
   What trials wait thor futur lives;
They'd elways keep this in thor view,
   To be gud men an' canny wives.
A yooth weel spent wad be thor aim,
   Then health an' peace wad close thor days,
They'd leave behint an honest nyem,
   An' prove 'twas wise to mend thor ways.
     Tyek maw advice, maw canny lad,
     Tyek maw advice an' mend yor ways.

THE CUDDIES AND THE HORSES.

A NORTHUMBRIAN DITTY.

Within a weel-knawn canny toon,
   In fact an ancient borough,
Alang whe's banks the Tyne runs doon,
   A stream baith deep and thorough.

And in this toon there dwelt a band
   O' men o' great resources;
And fate placed underneath their hand
   Some usefu' cairts and horses.

And ower abune this band o' men
   (This no the truth surpasses)
Were set a few, say five times ten,
   O' what we'll just ca' asses.

Thae last ransack'd the country roond,
  And myed a gran' selection;
Says they, we'll gie a thoosand poond
  And total jurisdection.

Yen Fowler ruled ower a', be reets,
  Yen Foulton did his biddens,
Yen Currie swepet out the streets
  And mucket out the middens.

Noo trams were laid, and men were paid,
  And streets they wanted sweepin';
And men were paid for nowt, 'twas said,
  And stories round were creepin'.

'Twas said that things were a' gaun wrang
  The workshop, tools, and pails, te,
Kept disappearin'; and, maw sang,
  Sae did the horses nails, te.

Up rose in rage thae asses then,
  That had seck great resources
(Aw mean thae fifty rulin' men
  That had the cairts and horses);

And in a language stern and strang,
  Demanded explanation,
And did at meetin's oft and lang.
  Myek deep investigation.

'Twas proved that maisters there were rizen
  That a' the men were maisters;
That wark for five was gien to ten,
  That a' alike were waisters.

'Twas proved, aye ower and ower agyen,
  Each followed his ain courses;
Each tried to leave the wark alyen,
  And only worked the horses.

The bipeds teuk their wark like play,
　And teuk their pay for nowt, noo ;
The horses, whey byeth neet and day
　Poor deevils they were rowt, noo.

But no thor fifty noisy men,
　Wi' a' their mighty pooers ;
They wadna work a day o' ten
　Much less o' " sixteen hooers."

And yet like asses hoo they brayed
　When pilferin' they suspected ;
Exposin' in their wild tirade,
　Hoo much they had neglected.

Then Coonsel White blamed Coonsel Black,
　And Black ca'd White a leear ;
Then a' agreed wi' happy knack
　That nyen frae blame were freear.

Aw've heerd o' horses rulin' men*
　And men bein' ruled bi lasses ;
But no till this day did aw ken
　O' baith bein' ruled bi asses.

Though Yahoos will be Yahoos still,
　And rin in crooked courses;
Yet cuddy asses never will
　Be fit te rule ower horses.

The moral that ye hev te draw,
　Frae a' that's herein spokken;
Is this—there is nae human law
　That isna sumtimes brokken.

But, should thae wyse puissant men,
　Wham ye hev placed in power;
Tyek oot a stinky hole, and then
　Just try and white-wesh 't ower ?

Newcastle, 1889.

* " Gulliver's Travels. "

GEORDIE'S JUBILEE ODE.

Hurrah ! yor Gracious Majesty, yor Jubilee hes cum,
An' wi' true Tyneside loyalty wor lads 'ill not be dumb ;
For England's hardy northern sons, tho' rough and rude
    wi' toil,
An' happier myekin' ships an' guns, or minin', still are
    loyal.

For fifty lang an' prosp'rous years wor monarch ye hev
    been,
An' monny a time in joy an' tears we've sung " God Save
    the Queen ; "
Se noo that we've been spared to see this prood an'
    happy year
We'll celebrate yor Jubilee wi' monny a hearty cheer.

Aw mind, when as a yung bit lass they placed ye on
    the throne,
Aw used te like yor bonny fyece that on wor coins wis
    shown ;
It seem'd se strange to see the wealth that fill'd the
    world wi' trade,
The British lion's power an' strength led biv a little
    maid.

Aw mind, tee, when Prince Albert sowt ye for his
    winsome bride,
Hoo ivvory Geordie, as he owt, rejoiced agyen wi' pride;
An' as yor little family grew, it pleased us all te see
Thor canny bits o' portraits, noo, a' cluster'd roond yor
    knee.

An' oh ! aw mind a bitter day that fill'd the land wi'
    gloom,
When gud Prince Albert passed away te fill an early
    tomb ;

An' England saw its widow'd Queen heartbroken an' in
tears—
Ah ! me, the sting o' that sad scene still lingers thro'
the years.

Aw mind, tee, when the Hartley Pit entombed two
hundred men,
Hoo wiv a muther's tender heart ye sorrow'd for them
then ;
The kindly letter that ye pen'd te bairns an' weepin'
wives
Wis read, an' read, an' read agyen, an' treasured a' thor
lives.

But life was not te be aal gloom for ye, wor noble Queen !
Imperial prestige com te croon yor royal state serene ;
An empire vast, throo-oot the world, noo answers te yor
sway,
Where Britain's glorious fiag's unfurl'd beneath an
endless day.

Arise, then, in yor majesty, wor Empress-Queen se
grand !
Ye rule the seas, the Colonies, an' India's princely land ;
Ye own anuther empire, tee, that fre' ye ne'er shall
part—
Ye own a People's Love, ye de !—the empire o' wor
heart.

God bless ye, Queen Victoria ! lang may ye live an'
reign !
Lang may wor coals an'. iron, tee, thor tip-top price
retain ;
An' while " Britannia Rules the Waves," united strang
an' free,
Her " Hearts of Oak" renown'd an' brave shall guard
yor Jubilee.

Newcastle, 1887.

A LETTER FRE GEORDIE ABOOT THE PRINCE'S VISIT.

Aw say, noo, Sir William, aw quite understand
Yor bringin' te see us a Prince o' the land—
A real livin' Prince that fre Sandringham hails;
Ne other, maw sangs! than wor awn Prince o' Wales.

Aw'll tell ye, Sir William, noo, what aw propose,
But, mind, what aw say is quite " under the rose;"
Some neet while he's here, tho' yor time's o' sum vally,
Ye might fetch him doon just te speak te wor Mally.

An' if ye'll bring win him the Princess o' Wales,
The wives in wor raw 'ill put on a' their veils;   .
The bairns wad be there, aye, reet doon te the twinnies,
Te offer thor Highnesses nice singin' hinnies.

Noo, canny Sir William, aw hope ye'll not snub
Wor Mally, for offerin' a tyest o' wor grub,
For mebbies the Princess would like, on the quiet,
Te judge for hersel ov a Geordie's rich diet.

Princeses, wi knaw, in fine dishes delight,   ,
But for me aw like sumthin' thet hes a gud bite;
An' nyen can beat Mall for a fat sma'-coal-fizzor,
Reed het fre the gordle te put in yor kissor.

August 15, 1884.

GEORDIE'S LAST ABOOT THE PRINCE.

Sir William, ye'll mind that aw wrote ye a letter,
An' aw've had ne reply, tho' it disn't much metter :
Ye mind that aw said when the Princes wis here,
They might gie us a call an' partake ov wor cheer.

If they'd cum, tho' wor raw's in a queer sort o' hole,
They'd hev fund we war clean tho' we wark amang coal.
Ay! wor clean an' wor civil, they'd hey tyekin' ne harm,
For wor coals may be het, but wor hearts are as warm.

H

Ov coorse for yorsel ye've a notion aw knaw
Ov th' oots an' the ins ov a colliery raw;
Hoo we leeve cheek-bi-jowl, an' wor wide open door,
Shews a gud kist o' drawers an' a clean sanded floor.

If the Princes had cum an' had ventured inside,
We'd hev shewn them wor "sticks" that's wor glory an' pride,
Wor French polish'd chairs an' wor fower powl bed,
An' wor bonny patch-quilt that we gat when we wed.

They'd hev seen, te, wor clock an wor sowin' machine,
An' a byekin' of breed that wis fit for a queen;
An' wor Mally aw'm shure, just for mensefulness syek,
Wad hev gien them thor teas an a nice gordle-kyek.

We'd hev shown them wor garden where often aw dig,
An' wor dyuks an' wor pidgins an' fat porky pig,
An' wor Belgian canary an' tortoise-shell cat;
An' maw tarrier dog shud hev worried a rat.

Noo, canny Sir William, the next time they cum
Let's hev ne Mayor's speeches, nor luncheons—by-gum!
For the way that they pulled them forst here an' then there,
Wis eneugh for te drive, aye, a Prince te despair.

August 29, 1884.

BLAYDON BURN.

In summer time maw heart dis yorn
Te hev a range throo Blaydon Burn ;
Thy rocky banks, se jagged and torn,
    Aw'm fond o' climbin, Blaydon Burn !

When harvest's cut and led away
And nicely stacked beside the hay
Then is the time te hev a day
    Amang thy brackens, Blaydon Burn !

Thoo's bonny in the buddin' spring,
When sangbirds myek thy welkin ring ;
But when the robin's in full swing,
    Thoo's glorious then, sweet Blaydon Burn !

Plash gans thaw wheel, O flinty mill,
Fed by the dam that leuks se still ;
Aw'm sure aw never gat maw fill
    Nor half enuff o' Blaydon Burn !

The stream runs ower its styenny bed,
Thro' monny a quiet neuk it's led,
Where fairies mebbies myek thor bed,
    Or dance all neet, in Blaydon Burn !

The smiddy-forge doon i' the dell,
(A rustic waif just like thysell)
If it could speak, aw warn't cud tell
    Some queery tyells, noo, Blaydon Burn !

What art thoo ? Glen, or dell, or burn ?
Thoo's aal and mair at ivery turn,
Whene'er aw leuk fresh beauty's born,
    An best iv all—thoo's Blaydon Burn !

One efterneun a bonny maid
Blackberryin on the banks she stay'd ;
An Elf, he saw her, so they said,
    And fell in love wiv Blaydon Burn !

At Path-head stile they used te meet,
And wander airm and airm at neet,
Throo pleyces varry wild, tho' sweet,
    In thy recesses, Blaydon Burn !

The lovers they were on the brink
Of gettin wed, but—sad te think !—
Some men wi' nets o' woven silk
    Snared the poor Elf in Blaydon Burn !

They've teun him wiv a goolden chain
Te toon wiv all his elfish train ;
He's garr'd te work wiv hand and brain,
    Far frev his hyem i' Blaydon Burn !

The waggonway's all groans and fears;
The varry wells run nowt but tears ;
The awd pit-shaft its vengeance swears
    Agyen thy robbers, Blaydon Burn !

The maid, she sits beside a thorn,
Frae late at neet till early morn,
And sighs, "Oh, when will ye return,
    Dear Elfin, back te Blaydon Burn?"

An echo comes upon the gale,
Borne softly up Tyne's lovely vale,
Glad-sons must rise when *Beacons-fail*
    Ere he comes back te Blaydon Burn!

SHE'S SUMBODDY'S BAIRN.*

One dark dorty neet, as aw myed me way hyem,
    Aw pass'd a bit lassie se bonny,
She belanged tiv a class that aw'm frightened to nyem,
    An' aw grieve that wor toon hes se monny.
She dress'd hersel' up in extravagant style,
    Wi' satins an' laces upon her;
As she passed me her fyece had a strange sort o' smile,
    That gliff'd me, it did, on me honour.
            Aw thowt, noo, that's sumboddy's bairn.

Aw wis struck bi her youth an' her bonny white skin,
    An' the bloom on her cheek, tho' 'twas painted,
As it flash'd on me mind, them's the trappin's o' sin,
    Oh, aw felt, aye, as if aw cud fainted.
Aw saw bi her walk, an' her heed toss'd se high,
    An' her artful-like manner se winnin',
Bi her ower-dress'd style, an' the glance ov her eye,
    That she'd myed, oh, that awful beginnin';
            An' aw thowt, noo, she's sumboddy's bairn.

* This touching piece was written shortly after the publication of
the startling disclosures of "Modern Babylon" in the *Pall Mall
Gazette*, which created such a sensation throughout the country some
few years ago.

O, lasses, remember yor feythers at hyem,
An' yor muthers, whe's hearts ye are breakin',
An' the brothers an' sisters yor bringin' to shyem,
An' the awful-like future yor myekin;
Divvent hanker for plissure nor dresses se fine,
Nor be tempted bi fashin an' beauty;
Think twice ere ye start on that dreadful decline
That leads ye fre' virtue and duty.
      Remember, yor sumboddy's bairn.

Ye lads, that a muther hes fondled an' nurs'd,
That hes sisters that's gentle an' pure,
Nivver lead a young lass in the way that's accurs'd,
Nivver breathe in her ear what's impure.
Reyther try to protect her fre' danger an' harm,
And if wranged, see the injured one righted;
For life hes been robb'd of its lovliest charm,
When a woman's fair fame hes been blighted.
      For mind, she wis sumboddy's bairn.

JOHN STOREY.

D'ye knaw John Storey? Yes, aw ken him weel,
A clivvor chep, besides a sonsie chiel,
A gentleman, and yet se kind and free,
He'll crack a joke wiv either ye or me.

Div aw ken John Storey? Man yor question's odd;
Div aw knaw·St. Nicklas'? says wor frind John Todd;
Aw ken him, and aw've knawn him frev a pup;
Not knaw John Storey? Wey aw browt him up!

There's not a pictor in maw hoose ye'll see
That's not John Storey's, except one—T.B.
Didn't Richardson declare, he's oath upon,
That only two could paint—he'sel' and John.

There's not a bonny place nigh hand wor Tyne,
But John hes painted, till it leuks divine;
His Awd and New Newcassel, leuk at them:
Not knaw John Storey? Man ye should think sheym.
Tom Richardsan's greet pupil: wey, ye clod,
Better say ye divvent knaw John Todd!

WOR TOON CLERK'S DEED.

Hang doon yor heed, wor canny toon,
And try wi tears yor grief te droon;
The tyrint Deeth hes struck him doon,—
    Wor Toon Clerk's deed!

His noble form we'll see ne mair,
Ye Cooncilmen, ye'll miss him sair;
O! sad, black year for Mr. Mayor—
    Wor Toon Clerk's deed!

Ye Magistrates upon the bench,
Deeth's cum yor purest leet te quench;
He's gien us all an awful wrench—
    Wor Toon Clerk's deed!

Oh, Tyne! flow slowly ower yor bed,
Yor awn, yor true commisshonor's dead;
Ye and yor streams yor tears may shed—
    Wor Toon Clerk's deed!

Ye friends that lure while health is here,
Be faithful still where death is near;
Upon his grave O! drop a tear—
    Wor Toon Clerk's deed!

If years of honest labour given,
In sturdy independence striven,
May fit a man for earth and heaven,
    May his indeed!

TOM'S WHITE CRAW.

Maw mate, Tom Softhead, when the days wis fine,
Thowt he wad hev a voyage upon the Tyne.
He myed strite te the Tyne Steam Ferry's boat
An' aboard the "Crawshay" he wis seun afloat.

As doon he sail'd, his pipe stuck in his jaw,
Thinks he, noo, this is just the "La-di-da"
If nobby swells wad real gud plesshur seek
They'd hev a sail like this myest ivvory week.

Tom thowt, noo, what a stream this Tyne mun be
Wiv its grand bridges and its noble quay,
Sic lots o' fact'rys, Ballast Hills a' green,
Docks, steeths and shipyards ne'er before he'd seen.

Noo, Tom read regularly the "Courant" news,
The births an' deaths an' Parlymentry views,
Thor "Multum-Parvo" an' thor Aad Records,
But myestly cared for bits on dogs an' burds.

He thowt hissel' a kind o' knawin' cove
That kenn'd a tomtit frev a cushey-dove,
For when a lad he'd often skinn'd his legs
Wi' climbin' trees for yalla yowley's eggs.

As tiv a landin' stage the steamer cam',
He heers a chep shoot oot "Tyne Dock," "Mill Dam,"
He just wis gan te shoot oot "Haud yor jaw!"
When ower his heed thor flees a greet white craw.

Away it sailed alang wi' lazy wing,
As like a "corbie," aye, as onnything;
Its size an' shape, an' greet lang neb an' a',
Tom nivver dooted but it wis a craw.

By gum! sais he, noo that's a curious thing
Te see a white black craw upon the wing!
Aa'll write the papers noo this varry neet,
An' tell them all about this wondrous seet.

When he got back, he tell'd a chep at hyem
Aboot the craw—but he myed nowt but gam,
An' swore, till he had seen the burd hissel'
His firm belief that Tom had had some yel.

Tom offer'd on the spot te stand the "batter,"
If he wad sail hissel' reet down the watter,
An' keep a gud look oot byeth high an' law,
As sure as deeth he'd see the white black craw.

The chep set off, an' varry seun wis back,
Wi' laffin', wey, his sides wis fit te crack;
"Wey, Tommy, man, thoo is a silly cull,
The white black craw is just a gray sea gull."

THE STORM WARNIN'.

O Geordie, lad, aw'm glad yor cum,
  Aw'm sure aw'm nearly driven frantic,
They say they've hoisted up the "drum"
  Te warn a storm fre the Atlantic.
O Captain Newton, canny man !
  Divvent keep us in commotion;
Try noo, maw hinny, when ye can,
  Te stop the storms fre ower the ocean,

Maw wife, she's sic a narvous sowl,
  She's elways shootin' oot, an' cryin'—
"Oh hear the winds, noo, hoo they howl,
  Anuther storm thor prophesyin'."
Aw sumtimes try te calm her doon,
  But she just says "Oh, had yor blether !
The warnin's oot, aw hear the soond,
  Wor gan te hev mair stormy weather."

She says, "Aw wonder how that man
  O' winds an' storms can aye be thinkin';
Can he not find some other plan
  Then set poor foaks's hearts a sinkin';
There nivver used te be sic wark
  When weather profits had ne callin',
But noo ne seuner is it dark
  But wor in dread o' chimleys fallin'.

Noo, Geordie, ye mun write the morn
  An' tell that bloomin' weather prophet
Aw'll give him'd het as sure's he's born
  If he storm tellin' dissent stop it.
Tell him his wind te blaw elsewhere,
  Sum other trade he'd best be larnin',
For if he gliffs us onny mair,
  Let him leuk oot—that's maw storm warnin'."

Newcastle, October 16, 1885.

THE "HEATHEN CHINEE" IN NEWCASSEL.

Oh, Sally, woman, hey ye seen
    Thor wonderful Chinee?
A shipload on them here thor's been
    Frae where they myek the tea.

They've cum to buy a ship, they say,
    An' greet big Airmstrang gun—
Thor in the toon myest every day,
    The folks hes had seck fun.

What gam it is te see them trail
    Aboot frae street te street,
Wiv blue bed-goons and lang pig-tail
    That hings doon te thor feet.

Aw wonder whe thor tyelior is—
    Thor breeks wad myek ye roar;
A reed sash for the waist-band dis
    The backside te the fore.

They've been tiv a' the shops, they say,
    For nicky-nacks and toys,
An' swagger roond the toon each day
    Wi' croods o' little boys.

They've been te th' Airt Galleree,
    An' mebbies te the play;
But what they think of ye and me
    Aw've nivver heerd them say.

But still thor very quiet sods,
    Although they leuck se queer—
Thor always full o' grins an nods,
    And never full o' beer.

Newcassel folks should treat them weel,
    And try and myek them stay:
They nowther swear, nor fight, nor steal,
    And elways seem to pay.

So all ye lads o' Coaly Tyne
    Let Chinese Johnny see
Yor nowther blackguairds, culls, nor swine,
    But decent Englishee.

Newcastle, 1881.

THE CHINESE SAILORS IN NEWCASSEL.

Air: "My Darling Molly."

John Chinaman hes cum te spy
  Wor canny Northern toon,
Wi' flatten'd fyece, an' funny eye,
  An' skin ov olive broon,
An' stumpy feet, an' lang pig-tails,
  An' claes o' clooty blue,
Alang wor street he slawly trails,
  Just like a live yule doo.

    John Chinaman, John Chinaman,
      What hev ye cum te see?
    What de ye think o' wor toon lads?
      Hoo de ye like wor quay?

Hev ye been te the Market yit,
  Wor cabbages te see,
Or "get a puddin' 'nice an het,"
  Or hev a cup o' tea?
Or hev ye been te the cutlers there
  Te get yorsel' a knife,
Or stroll'd the length o' filly fair
  Te choose yorsel a wife?

      John Chinaman, &c.

Or hev ye had a swagger doon
  By Mosley Street at neet,
An' watched them myek the bonny meuns
  Wiv Swan's electric leet?
Or hev ye been te Laws' place,
  An' smiled yor biggest laff,
An' let yor pig-tail hing wi' grace,
  Te get yor photograff?

      John Chinaman, &c.

Or hev ye been te Barkases,
   The bycicles te try,
An' show'd the Quayside marquises
   Like them yor rethor " fly ? "
Or hev ye been te see the shops,
   Te spend yor English tin,
An' as the money frae ye drops,
   Suspect yor tyek'n in?
        John Chinaman, &c.

Or hev ye had a ridey-pide   .
   Inside a tramway car,
Wi' grinnin' fyeuls at every side
   A' wundering what ye are ?
Or hev ye bowt a big ci-ga,
   An' tried te myek it leet,
An' gyen an' deun the La-di-da,
   Alang bi' Grainger Street ?
        John Chinaman, &c.

Then trail alang John Chinaman,
   Amang a crood ov bairns,
An' touchy tyesty all ye can,
   For that's the way one lairns;
But mind beware o' cheeky lass,
   An' whisky, John, and beer,
For if ye tyek an' extra glass,
   Oh, John, 'twill cost ye dear !
        John Chinaman, &c.

If ye shud tyek a drop ower much,
   An' it gets in yor eye,
An' ye get i' wor bobby's clutch,
   Ma sangs, he'll myek ye cry ;
He'll tyek ye up before the "chief,"
   An' though yor skin be broon,
An' ye be neither rogue nor thief,
   He'll fine ye half-a-croon.
        John Chinaman, &c.

But ye'll hev seen, John Chinaman,
    Barbarious English cheps,
Disgrace the vary nyem ov men,
    The blackguard jackanyeps !
Should ony drucken cuddy, John,
    Dar smite ye in the gob,
We'll let ye break a saucer, John,
    An' fine him forty bob.
                John Chinaman, &c.

John Chinaman, John Chinaman,
    Dressed in yor suit ov blue,
Ye've cum te see John Englishman,
    An' axee how-he-doo.
Yor welcome here, John Chinaman,
    Te buy yor guns an' ships,
An' if ye bring yor munny, John,
    Ye'll find us jolly chips.
                John Chinaman, &c.

JOHN CHINAMAN'S REPLY

(In Pigeon English)

To the Song "Chinese Sailors in Newcassel."

John Englishman he writee song which makee people smile,
And takee off John Chinaman in very funny style;
He makee fun of long pig-tail—me tink he better drop,
For English Johnny's hair am cut in style of " kitty crop."

John Chinaman he peaceable, and no mind bit of scoff;
But he no give "one on the eye," nor cut him pig-tail off !
Him do not sookey down him throat a lot of whiskey beer,
And then go knock him wifee down and frightful curse
    and swear !

John Englishman have whitee skin, but them him ways
    seem black ;
He kissee kindee one short time, then hit him friend hard
    smack.

And when you meet him in the street, or public house, or tram,

The only thing he seem to say am English for "go-tam;"

But still him am a regular brick and like him baccy chow,
But him a little much too fond of kickee up a row.

The English boys am very fast and makee somewhat free,

And shovee crowdee in the streets, and shout "here am Chi-nee!"

But this may be the customee in this barbarian land,

Where childe start the wax light trade as soon as him can stand.

Me like to talk the English tongue, though it be rather queer,

But me have learnt to say "by gum," "how-way," and "pint o' beer;"

I like to see John English in him skiff, when he "keel-rows,"
But hardly think it quite the thing to sit without him clothes.
But English swell dress very fine, him trousers very tight,
He gettee them for no sit down, him have to stand upright!

Him use himself for tailor's block, for so I've heard them say;

Him buy great many suits of clothes, but do he always pay?

He seems much proudee of his feet, and neatly them adorns;

John Chinaman's am not so smart, but then him have no corns!

When English Johnny want to ride him mount him bici-keel,

And look much like a monkey on him grandma's spinning wheel!

I likee your policemen, for he movee people on;
And rushee in to catchee tief when rogue am nicely gone.

I likee John Bull magistrate, he always home to dine;
And when the bobby bring him "case," he knowee how to "fine."

I like him grand pagodas where he 'vite him companee,
And ask him friend, John Chinaman, to " chin-chin " and
   to tea.

Him ladies voices very sweet, they have much pig-tail hair,
But oh, the style in which they dress, how much they do
   not wear !
I likee English grand big shops, fine windows looke well,
But customer am hardly sure, if he or goods am " sell ; "

I like much your joss houses, the music please mine ear,
But much I like your dram shop bar, your mild and bitter
   beer:
I likee much the Circus and reception givee me,
Ten thousand Tyneside Geordies shakee hands with John
   Chinee.

I likee much to welcome you on board the ship "Hae
   Shin "—
To see me use the chop-sticks and smokee and chin-chin;
And when I leave your canny Tyne, I'll kiss good-bye
   and laugh,
And wish your pretty girls were mine, and send them
   photograph.

MEG'S MISTEYK.

Meg Dodds an' her man wis sair doon i' the gob,
For weeks he'd been idle an' oot iv a job ;
The cupboard wis empty, the money wis dune,
An' another week's rent wad be due very sune.

She had been tiv her mother's (she leeved ower bye),
An' wis meykin off heym when a bill met her eye ;
For wi' leuckin an' seekin' for wark for her man,
She'd got in the way the shop windows to scan.

Is aw tell ye, not far frev her mother's she saw
A shop wi' fine bonnets set all in a raw ;
On the window wis plaister'd a paper quite thin,
" Wanted a Porter, enquire within."

Meg rushed away heym an' got Bill be the airm,
There's a chance for ye noo, man, some muney to airn;
It's a shop in the toon not far frae the clock;
It'll elways be better than wark in the dock.

Bill didn't much fancy't—in the toon he was shy,
But for seyk iv a job he wis willin' te try;
So he on wiv his jacket, an' off up the street;
Got engaged upon trial till the Seturday neet.

The forst thing he did wis te sweep oot the place,
Then te polish the windows, an' clean a glass case;
An' te get things put reet for the following day,
They gav him his tea a bit later te stay.

Noo Meg, she got thinkin' her Billy was lang,
And set off te the place to see what could be wrang;
She meyd te the shop where the paper had been,
And stood where she thought that she wadn't be seen.

The place wis all open, the gas all a-flare,
An' show'd her a seet that quite gav her a scare;
In the window quite plain, as she leuck'd throo the glass,
Her Billy she saw wiv his airms round a lass.

Wiv her heart iv her mouth, and her hands iv her hair,
The first thing she did wis te bubble and blare;
Her airms flew aboot like the wands iv a mill,
Then she dash'd at the window to get at her Bill.

"Thou villain!" cried she; "did thoo teyk me frae heym
Te insult me like this, and te bring me to sheym?
Thoo's just like the rest o' the men folk nee doot,
Thoo's not te be trusted, the moment thoo's oot.

Aw'll lairn thoo and others that women deceives
What it is te fall in wiv a gud pair o' kneeves,
An' the hussey that's wi thee, aw'll let ye beyth knaw;
Just let me get at her, her toppin aw'll claw."

She sprang throo the door, and gat Bill by the hair ;
He clung te the lass, and she leather'd the pair ;
Her dander wis up, so she meyd Billy roar,
And wi scufflin' they all landed doon on the floor.

The scene as they lay wis beyth funny and droll,
There wis Meg an' her man and a bonny wax doll ;
For Billy wis dusting the thing it appears,
And this was the cause of Meg's anger and tears.

She stared at the doll, and burst oot in a laff ;
For she saw she wis in for a stiff bit o' chaff ;
She kissed her poor man ; in confusion and shyem
She promised te nivver be jealous agyen.

Noo all ye young lasses afore ye get wed,
Myek yor mind up te trust in yor Bill, Jack, or Ned ;
For a draper's show figure wiv a cap on its head,
Needn't frighten a young married woman te deed.

OWT FRESH, HINNEY?

Oh, divven't say thor is ne news, thor's plenty, aw declare,
For truth an' lees iv ivvery kind are floatin' in the air;
Gan where ye will, see whe ye like, sum awful tyel they'll
    bring,
An' myek yor ivery hair stand strite aboot sum horrid thing.

Ye cannot buy a paper noo, nor waak alang the street,
But a murder or an ootrage yor benighted blinkers meet;
Sum greet hoose end wi' bills is cled wi' letters black an'
    white,
Detailin' shipwrecks, suicides, and findin' dynamite.

Wor elways on the " Ootlook," for " Advancin'," an' for
    " Joe,"
For " Whitten "-naryin' cawcussin' is noo the reglar go;
An' if ye want te spoil a man ye divven't like te call,
Spanghew him at a meetin' or placard him on a wall.

Ye divven't need te gan frae hyem sum awful news te get,
Thor's elways sum cat-astrophie yor quakin' sowl te fret;
Yor Cooncil's gyen te Parlyment wi' what they call a "Bill,"
Te sell ye te the doctors, or te Burke an' Hare, te kill.

They've gyen an' bowt awd Pandon, an' they've pull'd the
   myest on't doon,
An' spent a hundred thoosand just te get te Sandgate toon;
For week's they've had a dredger on the river hard employed
Te dig a greet big hole te droon byeth Hanlan an' Bob Boyd.

They've torned the Quay intiv a fair: on Sunday they begin
Te gammel wi' teetotums, an' the Swing Bridge roon' they
   spin;
They want te set the toon on fire, an' seun, on sum dark
   neet,
They'll bleeze up Earl Grey's Moniment wi' Swan's electric
   leet.

Thor's awful storms, they say, te cum; balloons, tee, gettin'
   lost,
An' tyels aboot poor fisher lads abused an' owerbord tost;
An' fights between the sowlgers an' Salvashun Armies, tee,
An' strikes an' horrid ootrages that terrify poor me.

Aw'm sure the world's just upside doon, an' things are aal
   gan rang,
Wor safe i' nowther train nor toon, wor life's not worth a
   sang;
They've flaid wor canny Queen away, the Parlyment's
   torned feuls,
Wor freedom noo they'll tyek away wi' Clotors an' Board
   Scheuls.

So divven't let us hear ye say thor isn't plenty news—
Thor manufactrin' 't ivvery day as weel as slaughterin' Jews;
If 'twasn't things is handy here—me baccy, beer, an' coal;
Aw'd emigrate this varry year an' leave this blissid hole.

I

THE WONDERFUL CURE.

One neet, noo, wor Sally was traikin',
When aw landed hyem efter dark ;
She said she felt all ower ackin',
Sais aw, wey it'll be the teuthwark.

The deevil teuthwark ye ! sais she, noo !
Sic' pains nivver ne body had ;
If they last onny langer aw'll de, noo,
Thor eneuf te drive onny one mad.

Hadaway noo, an' divvent stand dotherin',
Te the doctor's an' get me sum stuff ;
So aw off te the toon withoot botherin',
An' fetched her sum Handiside's snuff.

Aw sais, try that cure, noo, maw hinney,
While aw gan thee muther ti bring ;
Tyek a pinch an' aw'll fetch thee sum gin in,
If thoo'll leeve the frunt door on the string.

Her muther aw met cumin' ower,
So aw tell'd her hoo clivvor aw'd been ;
Ye shud hev seen hoo she did glower,
When aw tell'd her ne doctor aw'd seen.

Thoo villin' thoo's murdered maw dowter !
She hesen't been very lang wed ;
Varry likely the poother thoo's bowt her,
Will myek her be put tiv her bed.

Oh, crikey ! thinks aw, here's a case, noo,
If onnything happens poor Sall ;
The wumen they'll raise the hyel place, noo:
Aw'll he' te skeedaddle, that's all.

The fright set maw guts all a twistin',
Aw cuddent tell what for te de ;
At forst aw had notions o' listin',
Then aw thowt aw wad run off te sea.

Aw thowt aw wad just like te kiss her,
  Before her poor life shud depart;
For sairly aw knew aw wad miss her,
  The thowt on't myest broke me poor heart.

Aw myed for the door iv a trimmell,
  Expectin' te see her " laid oot;"
Aw heerd cups an' glasses gan gingle,
  Aw wis almyest for tornin' aboot.

Cum in, lad, an' leuk at yor Sally,
  Sais her muther all blushes an' grins:
On me dowter ye'll noo set a vally,
  See! she's bliss'd ye wi' two little twins.

Aw fund the snuff syef i' the bottel,
  It's cure she had ne need te try;
So aw poored sum gud gin doon me throppel,
  Seein' noo all me trubbels wis by.

WOR GRAND NEW RIVVER STATION.

O ! he' ye seen the landin' stage
  We've getten on wor Quay, noo,
The Tyne Steam Ferry's a' the rage
  Frev Elswick te the sea, noo;
Thor steamers, noo, they flee alang
  Fre' station on te station;
There's croods all gannin' noo, maw sang,
  For health and recreation.

Wor General Ferry bangs them a',
  Wi' boats se quick and smart, noo,
Thor grand new station fine an' braw
  Rejoices a' wor hearts, noo.
Noo lads and lasses, wives an' bairns,
  Myek all doon to the Quay, noo,
Byeth health and plissure ye will airn
  In a sail doon to the sea, noo.

There's nowt can beat wor bonny Tyne,
    It's a grand and noble rivver;
The wondrous seets the banks combine,
    Wey, man, a sail doon's clivver !
There's bridges, docks, an' a' se fine,
    An' ships frev ivvery nation,
An' mair, what caps wor coaly Tyne
    'S wor grand new Central Station.

And Jarra Slake will noo rejoice,
    An' se will aad St. Dunstan's,
An' Dent's Hole te will raise its voice,
    An' hail the Heworth grundstones;
An' Hawks's famous "twenty-fower,"
    That fla'd the hyel French nation,
Will wi' thor band be cumin' ower
    To glorify wor station.

THOR TAXIN' WOR DRINK.

Hang smash ! wey noo, Geordie, what think ye o' this
    That wor Government's gien us te chow ?
The Chancellor's Budget's a fyecer aw guess,
    An' alreddy it's raisin' a row.
They wanted sum brass, for thor heavy in debt,
    An' wor bund for te find them the chink;
Se for fear that the Russhins tiv India shud get,
    They've clapp'd on a tax on wor drink.

        Se for fear that the Russhins tiv India shud get,
        They've clapp'd on a tax on wor drink.

The grocers, ye knaw, hes been " clearin'" the tea,
    An' the baccy's been bowt bi the ton,
For 'twas thowt hevvy taxes laid on them wad be,
    An' on incomes, as sure as a gun.

But the Government kept ivverything tiv itsel;
Fre what's fair, wey, aw nivver wad shrink,
But te clap on a duty on whisky and yel—
Hang me ! wey that's taxin' wor drink.
But te clap on a duty on whisky an' yel—
Hang me ! wey that's taxin' wor drink.

The Budget, ye knaw, is the Government's till,
Where they stow a' the millions away,
An' when they want money thor pockets te fill,
Wey the Exchequer hes her te pay.
Se they get up a quarrel wi' Russia or France,
An' when wor at war's varry brink,
Wi' horrible stories they lead us a dance,
Then they clap on a tax on wor drink.
Wi' horrible stories they lead us a dance,
Then they clap on a tax on wor drink.

It's a blissin', though, Geordie, yor wages an' mine
Are byeth ower law te be taxed;
An' as we drink nowther sham-pagnie nor wine,
At thor duties we needn't get wax'd;
An' brandy an' sodda, and seccan like cheer,
Troubles nowther ov us, noo, aw think;
But if thor's a "meg" put on porter or beer,
We'll strike 'gyen the tax on wor drink.
But if thor's a "meg" put on porter or beer,
We'll strike 'gyen the tax on wor drink.

Aw lay, noo, when me an ye gans te the toon
An' wants owther suction or grub,
We'll hev te lay extra "cotterils" down
If we gan tiv a bar or a pub;
Dash me! but aw's reddy an' willin', is thoo,
Te teetotal them oot o' the chink?
Its "heeds or its tails" if we put on the "blue,"
They shannet tax us throo wor drink.
Its "heeds or its tails" if we put on the "blue,"
They shannet tax us throo wor drink.

If Gladstone wants money to get oot o' debt,
  Or te fight wi' the Russhian Bear,
Let him ax like a man, for we'll not see him beat,
  But he owt te de things " on the square."
It dissent need dodgin' an' threatenin' war,
  Te frighten us oot o' the chink,
But British taxpayers, tho' cuddies they are,
  'Ill not stand a tax on thor drink.

> But British taxpayers, tho' cuddies they are,
>   'Ill not stand a tax on thor drink.

May 14, 1885.

"SCOTCH HARES." *

TEUN : " The King of the Cannibal Islands."

Noo aal ye dainty foaks tyek care,
An' ov fine dishes noo beware,
The Fellin' foaks hev had a scare
    Wi' feastin' off Scotch Hares, man !
Doon yonder where there's lots o' Pats,
A drouthy dame hes dyeun the flats,
She's tyeun a rise oot ov the rats,
An' skinned a lot of awd Tom-cats.
Doon i' the cellar she wad sneak,
An' tice the pussies ivvery week,
She nivver ga' them time te squeak,
    But torn'd them te Scotch Hares, man !

Black cats an' white she sly'd away,
(One Tom wis worth a sov., they say)
Byeth yalla, tortoise-shell, and grey,
    She torn'd inte Scotch Hares, man !

* The origin of the above was owing to the circumstance that some party at the Felling had been guilty of killing and skinning some cats, and disposing of them as " Scotch Hares."—*Vide Daily Papers.*

The nybors wonder'd ivvery neet
They heard ne mew-maws in the street,
Nowt but the Bobby on his beat
Disturb'd thor slumbers a' the neet ;
But monny an awd maid lost her pet,
An' for her Tabby she wad fret,
Nor ivver thought that she was eat
  In a pie myed o' Scotch Hare, man !

Aw've heerd ov horses' flesh for food,
An' cuddies' te they say is good,
But cats aw nivver understood
  War ivver like Scotch Hares, man !
Noo sassages an' measly pork
May suit a German or a Turk,
But aw'm agyen sick squally work
As try poor pussy-cats te burk.
Noo ivvery time aw chance te hear
Maw inside squeak, aw'll feel a' queer,
An' if aw de aw'll shoot, oh, dear !
  Aw doot aw've had Scotch Hare, man !

Ye lads that's fond o' tarrier dogs,
An' like te hunt the moors an' bogs,
Yor better chasin' toads an' frogs,
  Than huntin' for Scotch Hares, man !
Tho' Tom-cats catterwaul on tiles,
Wi' yells that saints an' sinners riles,
Thor gyepin mooths like crocodiles,
Just myeks me twist maw fyece in smiles,
For oot o' bed aw slyly rise,
An' maw awd byutes aw at them shies,
But nivver will aw eat in pies
  Poor Tommies for Scotch Hares, man !

February, 20th 1885.

THE FELLIN' GHOST. *

Oh, hev ye heerd the jolly lark
    There's been doon at the Fellin', there;
The awful scenes that efter dark
    Hes gien the nybours sic a scare.
A lang white thing, in windin' sheet,
    That stalk'd about just like a post;
First up, then doon, then oot o' seet,
    For a' the world just like a ghost.
It fla'd them fre thor wits allmost,
Did this myest awful Fellin' Ghost.

The Fellin' foaks wis all distress'd,
    The apparition leuik'd se queer
The men an' wives they all confessed,
    They cuddl'd in for varry fear;
The noisy cats—thor call'd Scotch Hares—
    Gov ower thor squallin' on the tiles;
Spellboond, they couldn't smooth thor hairs,
    But silence kept all round for miles.
It fla'd them fre thor wits allmost,
Did this myest awful Fellin' Ghost.

The bairns in fear ran hyem fre schule,
    The gobby lads all said thor prayers;
The Bobbys' funk'd, the soapey culls
    War fritened o' the Ghost for fairs.

Considerable excitement was caused at the Felling a few years ago by what was supposed to be a ghost. It would try the doors and windows of houses about midnight, and finding them fastened, it would give an unearthly groan and then disappear. One of the residents, after his window had been shaken, gave chase with the poker, and finally run the supposed ghost into the police station.—*Vide Daily Papers.*

Neet efter neet, in wind an' storm,
    The awful spectre staalk'd aroond;
Wheivver leuk'd just saw the form
    Of ghostly white sail ower the groond.
It fla'd them fre thor wits allmost,
Did this myest awful Fellin' Ghost.

One chep, mair plucky than the rest,
    Lay wiv his wife all snug in bed,
When sumthin' on the door-sneck press'd,
    Says he, if that's the ghost aw'll he'd.
He oot o' bed as quick as thowt,
    An' teuk the poker iv his fist;
Says he, here goes, noo, neck or nowt,
    This ghost aw'll lay or aw'll be bliss'd.
It fla'd them fre thor wits allmost,
Did this myest awful Fellin' Ghost.

But Mistor Ghost wis ower real,
    An' sartin-ly it wasn't deed ;
For it seun let the poor chep feel
    A jolly whack upon the heed.
Ye mebbies divvent think its true—
    The Ghost went off at " double quick,"
The chep the phantom did pursue,
    Him wi' the poker, an' it the stick.
It fla'd them fre thor wits allmost,
Did this myest awful Fellin' Ghost.

Away they went wi' leet'nin' speed,
    White sheets an' sarks war fleein' sair;
Fre street te street the nybors seed
    Two ghost-like forms flee thro' the air.
At last the police station door
    Wis reached, an' in they byeth did call;
The Bobbys' taalk'd the metter ower,
    An' fund it was ne ghost at all.
But it fla'd them fre thor wits allmost,
Did this myest awful Fellin' Ghost.

TWENTY-FOWER O'CLOCK.

TUNE: "Polly's Nick Stick."

Smash marras ! hey ye heerd the tyel,
　That's gannin i' the toon, man?
Aw heerd it ower a pint o' yell,
　Aw had wi' Tommy Broon, man !
We just had gettin' sitten doon,
　It cam just like a shock, man—
They said the foaks in London toon
　War gan to double the clock, man !

Fal de dal, &c.

A chep wis readin' ower the news,
　Fra' Parlymint te sport, man !
He spell'd it oot wi' sairish tews,
　When sumthin' stopp'd him short, man !
He gav a shoot, and wiv a bang
　The tyeble he did knock, man !
Aw lowp'd reet up. Says aw, "What's wrang?"
　"Wey, Twenty-fower o'clock, man !"

"By gum!" says aw, "ye divvent say
　That sic a story's true, man !
An' that they'll coont the hoors a day
　I' scores, biv aal that's blue man?
The nine-hoors that we've had se lang
　They surely winnet dock, man?
Noo tyek maw word, thor'll sum get wrang,
　Wi' Twenty-fower o'clock, man !

Aw lay, noo, that they think wor skulls
　Wiv owt they'll easily prime, man !
They'll find they'll not, the slavvery culls,
　Knock us reet oot o' time, man !

Aw bet we'll knaw the time o' day—
  Sin Nicholas time, begox, man!
Wor buzzers, te, 'ill blaw away
  Thor Twenty-fower o'clocks, man!

Wor watches noo'ill a' be wrang
  Wor clocks mun change thor chime, man
Te strike the hoors 'ill tyek se lang
  They'll want thor owertime, man!
The varry ghosts that waalk at neet
  'Ill shiver at each knock, man!
When 'stead o' twelve, they end thor beat
  At Twenty-fower o'clock, man!

The railway trains 'ill not be last
  Aad Time they mean te beat, man!
Thor A.M.'s, P.M.'s noo are past—
  Ne mornin', neun, nor neet, man!
The drapers noo 'ill not dare squeak,
  But sadly show thor stock, man!
Wiv "early closin" all the week
  At Eighteen bi the clock, man!

Maw wife, she says, "Wey, hinney, Ned,
  Sic times aw've nivver seen, noo!
Te think o' puttin' the bairns te bed
  At quarter-past Nineteen noo;
Aw hope sic wark they'll surely snub,
  Maw feelin's it wad shock, man,
Te hey ye comin' fra yor club
  At Twenty-fower o'clock, man."

Says aw, "Oh divvent fear, maw lass,
  Te fret thor is ne caal, noo;
For when the Twenty-three hoors pass
  They cum te nowt at all, noo;
For twelve at neet's a cypher-ring,
  An' then the hoors they block, man!
So efter aal there's ne such thing
  As Twenty-fower o'clock, man."

On New Year's Eve we'll all be doon,
  As monny as ivver ye like, man;
Forst-footers frev all ower the toon
  Te hear the Major strike, man!
An' there we'll stand a gyepin' crood,
  Waitin' for his knock, man!
An' welcome in the New Year's Day
  At Twenty-fower o'clock, man!

THE CRAW'S NEST.

The erection of the Durham College of Science, at the Barras
Bridge, obliterated the well-known Lax's Gardens. The Grand Hotel
buildings also caused the removal of the tree and adjoining houses
known as the Crow Trees, *i.e.*, "Crow's Nest." This name arose
from the fact that for many years the crows nested in a large elm tree
that grew near the boundary wall, close to and overshadowing the
footpath. It was removed on the 28th February, 1889. Thirty years
ago crows were plentiful here and in St. Thomas's Church grounds.

Farewell, aad tree! where once the craws
  In times gyen bye did nest an' build;
Ne mair ye'll feel thor dusty claws
  Cling te yor branch, for noo yor kill'd.

When we were lads an' gan te skule,
  An' Eastertide wis drawin' near,
If we had nothin' new, we'd pull
  A fyece as lang as two, wi' fear,—

For we were warn'd, wi' solemn fyece,
  As we leuk'd up wi' friten'd gaze,
That if we hadn't sum new dress,
  The craws wad *notice*[1] wor aad claes.

Wor canny "Craw's Nest," lang ye've been
  A landmark for wor upper toon;
What changes in yor time ye've seen,
  An' noo they've gyen an' pull'd ye doon.

[1] There was a tradition among school boys that something new
in dress should be worn at Easter, otherwise the crows might besmear
their clothes.

When ye were yung, in times gyen past,
Newcassel then wis ony small;
Ne Grainger then his eyes had cast
Upon the " Major's " grunds an' Hall.[2]

The Lork an' Erick Burns[3] then ran
Where monks an' nuns myed thor retreats,
But "Dicky " com wi' magic wan',
An' changed them a' te noble streets.

Ay! in yor days o' saplin' green,
The Barras *bridge*[4] ye then cud see;
The Magdalen fields an' Pandon Dene
Wad all be country then for ye.

St. James's[5] an' the miller's pond,[6]
An' Lax's Gardens, nigh ye laid;
The Pedlar's Raw[7] wis just beyond,
An' ower fornenst, the New Parade.[8]

[2] The "Major's" grounds and hall, Anderson Place, stood near Lambton's Bank, formerly the monastery of the Franciscan, or Barefooted Friars, purchased in 1834 by Richard Grainger for his grand improvements.

[3] The Lork Burn ran down the lower part of what is now Grey Street, and through the middle of Dean Street to the Sandhill; it appears to have been a continuation of the Darn Crook. Erick Burn crossed New Bridge Street, and ran by way of Erick Street to Stockbridge.

[4] Fifty years ago the Barras or Barrows Bridge. crossing the Baillie burn, was quite visible just beyond the present Post Office. It was rebuilt, raised, and widened in 1818. The Miller's Cottage still stands, adjoining the arch, with iron rails round it; it is three feet below the present street level. [Now rebuilt.]

[5] St. James's stood on the site of the present Museum. There was once a chapel here (St. James's Kirk). It once bore the name of Sick Man's Close.

[6] The Miller's Pond was just at the foot of Eldon Street; it intercepted water from the Baillie Burn for the Barrow's Mill. In 1651 it was called Bare's Mylldam. The water mill is said to have belonged to the Blackfriars.

[7] Pedlar's Raw, a portion of Northumberland Street, opposite Ridley Place, said to have been built by a successful pedlar.

[8] The "New Parade " (Haymarket) in Percy Street was opened in February, 1808. The Newcastle Volunteers were inspected there by Col. Hawdon. They were previously drilled in Blackett's Field.

The Baillie Burn[9] wis open then,
  Where oft we plodg'd wivoot wor shoos;
It's closed, an' Mr. Race[10] is gyen,
  Wiv all his milkwives an' thor coos.

Aad Sidgate,[11] ay! an' Bruce's skule,[12]
  Wad once be knawn as local nyems;
But noo the bonny Dene's all full,
  An' all aroond ye's bricks an' styens.

Ne doot ye'll mind—tho' lang ago,
  Afore that sum iv us wis born,
The " Wonder " coach, or " Tally Ho,"
  Cum rattlin' by wi' bugle horn.

But noo the chatterin' o' yor craws
  Wad scarce be heard for trams an' trains,
An' ne one cares—an' fewer knaws,
  What's cum o' yor poor last remains.

But nivver mind, poor aad Craw tree,
  Ye an' yor nests may pass away,
But roond the place ye used te be,
  Yor nyem will linger monny a day.

For trees, like men, mun cum an' gan,
  Sum spot awhile they may adorn,
But true te Muther Natur's plan,
  Thor here the day, an' gyen the morn.

Newcastle, Feb., 1889.

9 The Baillie Burn crossed the Barras Bridge from Eldon Street
into Pandon Dene.

10 A well-known and enterprising dairyman and farmer, at the
entrance to Sandyford Lane, whose fine herd of milch cows and
excellent byres were the admiration of everyone. The milkwomen
started on their rounds with huge cans of milk on their heads.

11 Sidgate, or Sidegate, the ancient name of Percy Street.

12 One of the celebrated academies of Newcastle, founded by Mr.
John Bruce, and conducted for many years by his son, the Rev. J.
Collingwood Bruce, the learned antiquary and author of the " Roman
Wall." Many of the business men and prominent citizens of the
town received their education at this school. The house stands at
the corner of St. Thomas' and Percy Streets, and is now occupied as
a steam laundry.

OH, MY! WHAT CHANGES.

Oh, dear, hoo things hes altered noo,
  Since trains an' trams war started;
If wor gran-dads war livin' noo,
  Maw sang, they'd be divarted.
Wor gud aa'd times are past an' gyen,
  We often treat them scurvy;
Te get a new sensation noo,
  We turn things topsy-torvy.

In owlden days wor fethers yews'd
  Te ride on shanky's naigee,
An' a' the ilks they ivver knew
  Wis teuthwark an' the aigee.
They didn't smoke cut cavendish,
  Nor cigarettes for baccy;
Nor christen bairns a lot o' nyems,
  But just plain Tom an' Jacky.

We divvent noo wesh claes at hyem,
  We send them te the laundries;
An' boil worsels in Turkish baths,
  Till wor like salamandries.
Wor not content wi' Tinmuth noo;
  Te join amang the dippers,
But rush about like scadded cats,
  Excursions an' cheap trippers.

In owlden times wor wives an' men
  Cud work in real gud fashun,
But noo wor time we myestly spend
  In billiards, bools, an' mashin'.
We didn't lairn a lot, that's true,
  Nor hev ne schule bord capers,
But nowt gans doon but morals noo
  Wor fed on comic papers.

THE COMET.

Bygum, noo, aw say, he' ye heerd o' the star
That's fetched a' the wives an' the bairns te the door,
An' what d'ye think thor aal glow'rin' for ?
　　Whey just for the wunderful comet.

Leuck thonder ! aw leuck'd but nowt could aw see,
But a weeny bit star just the size ov a pea ;
Ses aw, noo, had on ! divvent ye gammon me,
　　Aw divvent beleeve in yor comet.

Ses they, wey thor's word all the way fre Brazeel
That's gi'en all the quidnuncs a funnyish feel,
They say that we'll mebbies get sent te the deil
　　If we divvent keep cleer o' the comet.

Aw myed me way hyem in a flutter at neet
Te fetch oot the wife for te leuck at the seet,
Hoot man, noo, she ses, wey ye cannot be reet,
　　Whe cares for yor wunderful comet ?

Ses aw, wey maw lass, noo, then d'ye not knaw
Thor the queerest like creeturs that ivver ye saw ?
They've heeds, aye an' tails, mebbies legs te an' a',
　　Thor wunderful things are the comets.

But onyhoo mind aw'm not in for a row,
For Barkas aw'm tell'd hes the hyel thing in tow,
An' he knaws weel a star frev a pig, noo, aw vow,
　　Se aw'm sure it's a wunderful comet.

Get oot, noo, ye fondy, ses she, had yor ways,
Aw divvent beleeve the one half that he says ;
It's mebbies a fad like his new fashioned claes,*
　　So it's aal in me eye, is the comet.

He needn't set up for a new weather clark,
An' spy throo lang glasses at neet efter dark ;
It's mebbies a rocket escaped fre the Park,
　　An' the fondy's mistyend for a comet !

* An exhibition of ecclesiastical vestments held in the Art Gallery.

HALLIDAY-TIME.

The fact'ry's are closed, an' wor wark is laid in,
An' it's close upon halliday-time,
An' we've getten wor bottles o' whisky an' gin,
An' wor pork an' wor gyeuses se prime;
An' we've bowt worsels misseltoe, holly, an' fir,
An' wor myekin yule-doos in gud time;
For wor folks is detarmined te hev a greet stir
An' be menseful at halliday-time.

We've been syevin' up hes wor Geordie an' me
Te gie' wor aa'd folks a bit treat;
We've bowt them sum corrins an' baccy an' tea,
An' we've laid in a great lump o' meat.
The aa'd wife she's ordered the things fre' the Store,
An' she'll myek singin-hinnies se prime;
For we mean te hev liquor an' grub in galore,
An' be menseful at halliday-time.

We've sent doon te Waalker for Sally an' Joe;
(He's maw mate, an' aw's on for the lass),
An' me Aunt an' me Uncle fre' Quality Row,
For thor byeth on them fond ov a glass;
An' Father's aa'd chum whe the fiddle can play,
While we join wiv a little bit rhyme;
For we all like te meet on a Chrissamas Day
An' be menseful at halliday-time.

Se onny aad freen's fra the country or toon
That shud happen te dander wor way,
They'll be welcome, aa's sure, just te gie's a caal roond
If they like on the Chrissamas Day.
Wor sure to be in, for it's elways wor plan
Te keep up aa'd customs se prime,
An' myek wor freen's jolly an' de aal we can
Te be menseful at halliday-time.

K

Aa've bowt lots o' papers wi' pickturs an' tyels
    An' sum toys for the nybor's bit bairns,
For aw think it's the best to be happy worsels
    An' de gud wi' the munny one airns.
Besides, when yor gannin' te *pop* te yor lass
    It's as weel te hev ivvry thing prime,
For she mebbies might rue if one let the chance pass
    Te be menseful at halliday-time.

Aw've getten me photygraf tykin' bi Laws
    Te put in wor album se fine,
An' mebbies they'll sell them at Allans', whe knaws,
    For wor gud luckin' cheps on the Tyne.
An' when aw get spliced an' a hoose o' me awn,
    The *Northumbrin'* might print us in rhyme,
For its artist's a brick, and it's jolly weel knawn
    That he's menseful at halliday-time.

December 14, 1883.

THE GLADSTONE CRAZE.

Noo this is the thing that surprises me,
    An' hes deun for several days,
Is hoo wor north-country cheps can be
    Se bit wi' the Gladstone Craze.
There's nowt a man's not willin' te de,
    When party-spurrit runs high;
He sinks his faith an' his principles te,
    Te shoot his political cry.

        Ov all the things that surprises me,
            Is a man's political ways;
        If Liberal he, aw'm Liberal te,
            But not bit wi' the Gladstone Craze.

There's monny a decent fellow aw knaw,
That works for his daily breed,
That reeds, aye, an' thinks, an' is what aw ca'
A sensible fellow indeed.
But onny just touch his political place,
Hoo his dander gits up, noo, maw sang!
An' tho' ivvery day brings another disgrace,
Sweers Gladstone cannit de wrang.
Noo this is the thing that surprises me,
Ne metter what Gladstone says,
It's Gospel, suppose it's a thumpin' lee,
'Caws he's bit wi' the Gladstone Craze.

When dynamite shivers wi' dreadful boom
An' gi'es us the horrors wi' fear, .
An' wi heer fresh disasters at far Kartoom,
Wey, wor apt te feel awfully queer.
But nowt wor Grand Owld Muddler scars,
Supremely contented is he;
While the nations abroad are preparin' for wars,
He's at Ha'arden "fellin' a tree."
Noo this is the thing that surprises me,
Ne metter for Gladstone's ways,
Ne wrang can *he* de, ne wrang can *they* see,
'Caws thor bit wi' the Gladstone Craze.

Tho' Germany collars a colony here,
An' France tries the same little game,
An' Russia lays hands on Herat—varry near—
An' the Soudan's a blunderin' shame;
Just then G.O.M. hes te gan te the play,
An' in comedy laff off his cares;
While the nation te war an' sedition's a prey,
He's at Ha'arden "readin' the prayers."
Noo this is the thing, an' a corker te,
Ne metter hoo Gladstone prays,
He cannot myek wrang appear reet te me,
Aw'm not bit wi' the Gladstone Craze.

Newcastle, 1885.

MICKEY AN' THE M'YUN.

Wor Mickey had been on his club meetin' neet
Enjoyin' his usual annual treet,
Wi' smokin', and drinkin', and monny a nicker,
He'd managed te swally a canny sup licker.

He'd heard a chep argy " bi' this an' bi' that,"
That the earth wassint roon', but was perfectly flat;
" An' if he had time, he was sure he was yeble,
Te prove it wis like wor mahogany t'yeble."

As he pletted his way on the road tiv his h'yem,
Defyin' the world te say " that " tiv his n'yem;
An' wis just gan te call the " earth flattener " fond,
When he saw the m'yun's f'yece shinin' doon iv a pond.

He stopp'd an' he stared, in a kind iv a fright,
Confoonded wiv such an unusual sight;
" Begox noo," ses he, " but here's news for the toon,
Aw declare, if the m'yum hessint tummil'd reet doon."

He gethored his thowts, and he muttered " maw sang—
But that roondiflat chep hessint been se far wrang;
Aw'll bet what ye like, the orth's dragged hor small kedge,
An' the m'yun's missed her mark, an' dropp'd ower the
        edge.

Smash man ! for a heuck, or a net, or a gun,
Aw'd strip off an' dive, or aw'd fish for that m'yun ;
It wad be a fake, wor next heed meetin' neet,
If wor club pitch'd the gas, and went in for m'yun leet."

He ran roon' the pond, but whereivvor he went,
She seemed te slip frev him, till he was fair spent ;
While wipin' his f'yece, an' " hang-smashin' " his eyes,
He sees the real m'yun shinin' up i' the skies.

" Aw'll be blissed, noo," ses he, " did ye see owt like that,
I'st the orth or mesel that's the darnderest flat ?
Whichivvor it is, aw can tell thoo freend m'yun,
Thoo's gien Mickey Proddles a jolly good run."

WOR FREE LIBORY.

The Libory's open, noo, they say,
  Aw went te hev a l'yuk,
Aw thowt there wad be nowt te pay,
  An' ax'd them for a b'yuk.

" A b'yuk, young man?" ses they te me;
  Ye'll hev te write yor n'yem;
An' ye mun pay a penny te,
  An' prove ye leeve at h'yem.

" At h'yem," ses aw! " whey de ye think
  Aw've drop'd doon fra the sky?
Me n'yem aw divvint mean te blink,
  They call me Tommy Spry.

But what's this silly nonsense for?
  A b'yuk aw've cum te seek; "
Ses he, " Maw man ye'll get the door,
  If ye gies onny check."

Aw dash'd maw coat upon the grund,
  An' rowl'd maw sleeves up tight;
Ses aw, " Or at the door aw'm fund,
  Aw mean te show ye fight."

Wi' that the Libory gaffer cum,
  Ses he, " What's aw this sang?"
Aw tell'd me t'yel, an' wiv a hum,
  Ses he, " Maw freend yor wrang.

Te setisfy the public need,
  Wor t'yekin' ivvory pains;
An' though we len' ye b'yuks te read,
  We cannit len' ye brains.

So sit ye doon upon that chair,
  An' scan the Burgess List,
Yor n'yem an' number 'ill be there,
  Unless they've b'yeth been miss'd.

An' if its reet, cum back next week,
  Yor ticket then aw'll write;
But when ye cum yor b'yuk te seek,
  Mind divvent cum te fight."

THE BETTOR TIMES THAT'S CUMMIN!

TUNE: "Because he was a Bonny Lad."

Noo men and maisters, brothers all,
Thor's been a greet depression;
That British trade hes had a fall,
Thor needs ne big expression;
    But sure aw am that times 'ill mend
    And wark 'ill sune be plenty;
    Locks-oot and strikes 'ill hev an end,
    And all the ills they've sent ye.

Noo when aw think of all that's bye—
The trouble and vexation;
And hoo wor hardy sons did try
Te win throo Arbitration;
    Ses aw, whey England's not the place
    For men te turn thor back on;
    Gyen foreigners sure we'll win the race,
    In spit o' them they crack on.

Wor wages cannot lang bide doon,
The world mun aye be waggin,
And as the coin gans roon' and roon'
Sum share on't we'll be baggin.
    Canadians, if they like, may cum
    And try te beat wor scullers,
    But "Yankee Doodle's" not the teun
    Te which we'll strike wor cullors.

Come then, me lads, tegither pull,
And join yor canny maisters;
Yor shops wi wark 'ill sune be full,
And cash for stomach plaisters;
    Stick te yor wark, like Britons true;
    Be honest in yor stations;
    Te be the best, keep that in view;
    Then fear nee uther nations.

The world at lairge te tax wor guds,
Tegither may be banded,
But, wiv freetrade and brotherhood,
We'll fight them single-handed.

The farmer's had his wark in hand—
Low prices and bad seasons;
But let him biv his landlord stand,
And ply him wiv gud reasons.

When ivery rood o' British soil
Biv owners is regarded
As held in trust, then prudent toil
Will always be rewarded;
We'll eddicate and try te lairn
The laws o' trade and science;
An honest pund we'll always airn
Wiv pluck and self reliance.

Then as a nation brave and strang
We'll turn a new leaf ower;
We've followed fulish schemes ower lang
Tiv loss o' wealth and power.
Iv Russians, Turks, and wild Afghans,
And Zulus, fierce and mighty,
Frev all such like we'll wesh wor hands
And mind worsels in eighty.

Wor rulers they'll provide gude laws,
Wor sowljers guard wor honnor;
We'll all support wor country's cawse,
Nyen shall throw dort upon her.
·Then peace will reign, industry's wars
We'll amicably settle;
United, free frev party jars,
We'll wark wor coals and mettle.

Noo, hip-hooray! for prosperous times,
And better years that's cummin;
Hammers 'ill ring like merry chimes.
Industry's bees keep hummin'.
Then farmers, tradesmen, warking men,
Tegither raise yor voices,
Cheer! for the times 'ill come agyen,
That surely shall rejoice us.

From the North of England Almanac for 1880.

A NEW START FOR EIGHTY-ONE.

Last year aw thowt the tide had turned,
And that success we'd fairly earned;
That all wor troubles in the past,
Tho' for wor gud, war gyen at last ;
That noo we'd hear the pleasant sang
Of buzzar's soond and hammer's clang;
That want and tears wad flee away,
And wark and brass wad win the day.

That health and wealth wad smile aroond,
And joy in every heart be foond;
That farmers wad wi' pleasure till,
While gowlden grain thor barns wad fill;
That trains ashore and ships at sea
Wi' merchandise wad loaded be ;
That men wad fairly work the day,
And hev full draws at ivvery pay.

That trade wad thrive in ivvery street,
And shops wad blaze wi' cheerful leet;
That folks in scores wad come te toon
And myek the glitterin' coin flee roon' :
This might hev been had we been wise,
And syeved when things wis on the rise,
And had but thowt te lay away
A trifle for "a rainy day."

Then come, me lads, let's hev a try
In *Eighty-One* success te buy ;
Wi' hopeful hearts and willin' hands,
Let's all obey the just demands
Of social and religious laws,
Ordained in civ'lisation's cause;
Wiv industry and prudent thrift
Let's gie wor trade a hearty lift.

One simple cure aw fain wad press—
Let's gamble, smoke, and drink the less;
We needn't wear sech costly claes,
Tho' that's not what the tyelior says;
He likes te see ye weel put on
If ye've got cash te wark upon;
Aye, *Ready-Money*—"there's the rub,"
Wiv that, ye need te ax ne "sub."

Then, in yor sphere, tyek proper rank,
And start at once the *Savings Bank;*
Then fortin'—aye, and freens—'ill smile,
And comfort te will bliss yor toil;
Wi' freens and fortin' comes good nyem—
Wi' comfort comes a *Happy Hyem;*
If comfort, freens, and fortin' cheer,
These sure will myek a *Happy Year.*

From the North of England Almanac for 1881.

THE REET AND THE WRANG.

TUNE: "Paddle your own Canoe."

Whatever ye de, as life's changes ye see,
  Let the journey be short or be lang,
May yor rule elways be to be jovial and free,
  Myekin freens wi' the reet, not the wrang.

When yor young and at schule, divvent practice the fule,
  Nor yet join wi' the frivolous thrang ;
If yor talents be dull, at yor beuks tyek a pull—
  Elways choosin' the reet frae the wrang.

While lairnin' yor trade, nivvor let it be said
  That ye're one o' the " skulkin' gang :"
And nivvor be flai'd, if a man ye'd be made,
  Te de reet, aye, in spite o' the wrang.

If a sowljer ye be, or a sailor at sea,
  In battles an' billows amang,
Deeth's bullet may flee, or the wave "swallow thee,"
  If ye're reet, then they cannot come wrang.

If ye follow the plough, tend the horse or the cow,
  Or the sheep ye should labour amang;
If ye reap or ye sow, aal yor labour bestow,
  That the reet may ootnumber the wrang.

If ye work on the line, or yor doon the deep mine,
  Where life isn't worth an aald sang,
For yor sake and mine nivvor duty resign,
  Then ye'll elways be reet, an' not wrang.

If ye're placed in a bank, or wi' noblemen rank,
  Or can boast ov a predigree lang,
Yor life's but a blank if yor morals be " crank,"
  For it's reet ye should nivvor de wrang.

Should ye wield the greet pen, or hev rule ower men,
  Through the press or industry's thrang,
Be diligent then—yor whole power te len'
  That the reet may aye conquer the wrang.

If trouble be sent where a blissin' was meant,
  Through the weather or trade hingin' lang,
Return what was lent, an' withold not the rent,
  For it cannot be reet te de wrang.

If a Lib'ral suits ye, an' a Tory suits me,
  Nivvor stoop te political slang;
"The voter that's free, an' my country for me,"
  An' surely that's reet an' not wrang.

If England we see, bravely strivin' te be
  A pattern the nations amang,
Her fleets on the sea settin' slavery free,
  An' her airms ne'er engaged in the wrang.

While nations aroond are in tyranny foond,
  Where the weak hes te kneel te the strang,
Then in "honour wor boond" te declare, as we've foond,
  That she rules for the reet, not the wrang!

From the North of England Almanac for 1881.

FREE TRADE OR FAIR?

The year cums in, the year gans oot, and leaves us much
the syem;
And tho' things seem te change aboot, they only change
in nyem;
Yet still another change may cum, a change aw'd like te see,
Though, strange te say, not lik'd biv sum—" That trade
be Fair and Free."

We started weel sum years ago, and byeth bi' land and sea,
Owld English pluck wis never slow te show what it cud de;
Wor Arkwrights and wor Stephensons, true heroes we may
call,   [ov all.
Whe's genises for wor commerce won the foremost place

In every branch iv human airt, in farmin' and in trade,
We elways teuk a leadin' pairt, and fame and fortun made;
While uther countries roond aboot teuk lessons frae wor
skill,
And till they fund wor secret oot, professed at least gudwill.

But this is where the pinch begins: we made wor trade
se free,
That forriners wis welcomed in te sell te ye and me;
But when we'd paid for what we'd got, and wanted them
te buy,
They turned upon us like a shot and raised thor tariffs high.

We tell'd them all what Cobden said, and Stuart Mill and
Bright—
What sacrifices we had made te start free trade ootright;
And reason'd, as we'd gyen se far, the least that they cud de,
Wis just te put us on a par and let wor goods in free.

" Nay, nay," said they, " That wadn't de; wor bund te
mind worsels,
Mere trade's not much, hooever free—it's profit, man that
tells !
And if we didn't mind wor eye wor trade wad sune be gyen;
Then, wi' ne trade and all te buy, whey profit there'd be
nyen.

Wi' treaties an' wi' bounties we can bowlster up wor trade,
And try and undersell ye in the markets that ye've·made;
Free trade's an English hobby, and ye've gien'd a tidy spell,
And if it hesen't paid ye, ye can only blame yorsel."

Thinks aw, whey noo there's sumthin' in what Mr. French-
    man says;
The only trade worth dein in is trade that really pays;
Cheap labour and lang oors wi' them hes gien them seck
    a pull,
That wi' protected trades at hyem they undersell John Bull.

Free trade's a canny thing we knaw : it's dune a bit o' good;
It's brought doon prices nice and law, and cheapened a'
    wor food;
But then it should be free all roond, that all alike might
    share,
A trade like this wad then be foond not only free but fair.

Noo let me ax ye workin' man that lives bi toil and trade,
Just tell me straight, noo, if ye can, what things are English
    made?
For mind ye, what ye divvent myek in food, or drink, or
    dress,
Is that much off the British kyek and makes yor wages less.

Yor joiner work frae Belgium cums—yor iron work as weel;
And France sends sugar, silks and wine, and Prussia sends
    ye steel ;
And one bi one the nations roond are poachin' on yor grund,
And stealin' byeth yor trade and tools whereby yor bread
    wis fund.

But warst is free America, that frae worsels hes sprung,
That's dune a bit for freedom's day, and speaks wor muthor
    tongue;
She's turned ageyn her parent land, and painful te relate,
Though we give her a free trade hand, she'll not reciprocate.

Noo, if sum folks will stupid be, or selfish, or unkind,
And close thor ports te ye and me—they may if se inclined;
We'll deal wi wor awn Colonies and every friendly state,
But on thor heavy tariff-ees, whey we'll retaliate.

We'll try and win wor honours back for quality and style,
And prove we hevent lost the knack wi' hammer and wi' file;
And if wor standard be A1, iv trade we'll get wor share,
But this we will insist upon—free trade all roond and fair.

From the North of England Almanac for 1882.

WOR CIVILIZATION !

TUNE: "Canny Newcassel."

Noo civilization's a queer sort o' thing,
　　It's constantly myekin' a noise ;
It boasts the millenium it's gannin' te bring,
　　And all sorts o' plissures and joys.
It talks aboot myekin' folks all iv one mind—
　　That the rich an' the poor shall agree
Te share wiv each uthor an' kiss-an'-be-kind,
　　In a new kind o' felicitee.

It's always declarin' through pulpit an' press,
　　That its objects are noble an' gud ;
But its preechin' an' practiss aw'm bund te confess
　　Are hardish te be understud.
It talks aboot justice, an' morals, an' truth,
　　An equality, freedom, an' health ;
But while it dis this it keeps twistin' its mooth,
　　An' scrapin an' booin' te wealth.

It sends pioneers te the lands far away,
　　Where there's Blackeys, an' spices, an' goold ;
It tells them thor heathen, an' lairns them te pray,
　　And myeks them submit te be ruled.

Of coorse the poor blacks little wisdom hev got,
  And wad eat a white man like a bun ;
Then civilization says, let them be shot,
  For it elways gans airm'd wiv a gun.

At hyem it keeps talkin' o' commerce an' trade,
  And economy, duty, an' law ;
But it sticks to the brass till it's fortin' is made,
  Then it sets up for lairnin' an' jaw.
And religion and politics mun hev a place
  In the national "Juggernout Car ; "
But, while it keeps pratin' o' gudwill an' peace,
  Its mebbies preparin' for war.

Each civilization believes in a cry,
  And follows the bellwether's lead ;
Its Tory or Whig, or its low church or high,
  And sweers biv its party an' creed.
For each one believes it can swagger an' boast
  And all other systems run doon,
And while thor contendin' whe shud "rule the roost,"
  Thor victims may wander or droon.

Then all kinds o' notions get shoved to the fore,
  Under civilization's fine nyem;
Channel Tunnels or Land Acts, neer heard on before—
  Aye, or Clotures, it's all just the syem.
Some giant concocter gets haad iv a scheme,
  An' wi' money, or cheek, or address,
Contrives te foist off (his) un-limited dream
  As the latest grand march in progress."

Then there's some tyeks a fancy for "free or fair trade,"
  And others "protection " 'ill try ;
And as lang as they find plenty money is made—
  Wey, then "principle's " all-in-me-eye.
And so on all ower whereivver ye be,
  There's some folks thor hobbies will air,
But trust them wi' power, they'll sune let ye see
  What for civilization *they* care.

But the civilization that bothers me most
   Is the kind that *will* run inte debt ;
And when it shud pay winnet come te the post,
   But hes talent te always forget.
That ties all it can an' then thinks it gud sport,
   When it finds ne mair money ye'll lend,
Te hev a "whitewesh" in a bankruptcy court
   Wiv its "trustees" and ne dividend.

Noo surely it's time we teuk'd inte wor heed,
   Te leuk civil shams in the fyece,
And reckkon up where an' te what they may lead,
   Before we get inte some mess.
For "righteousness" nations an' men can exalt,
   But folly brings byeth te sad ends;
If wor civilization be not in the fault,
   It an' virtue should always be friends.

Then let's all contrive as we journey through life,
   Te be guided bi principles true,
And te keep on good terms wi' the "world an' his wife"—
   It's the way te get plissantly through.
For it isn't much use gannin' in for fine nyems,
   If uther things dissent agree;
Plenty wark an' good money, an' clean happy hyems,
   Is the civilization for me.

From the North of England Almanac for 1883.

THE WONDERFUL THINGS O' THOR
MODERN DAYS.

Tune: "Weel Dune Cappy."

Noo events keep changin' and choppin' aboot,
We nivvor knaw what's the next thing te cum oot;
On wonders and horrors we constantly sup,
And as sune as one's gyen then another crops up,
   Till wor all in a dother, an' a reglar bother,
   Wi' the wonderful things o' thor modern days.

Things noo are quite different te when we were bairns.
And its awful the things that wor bowdckites lairns;
One officor tyeks them te schule evvery day,
And another one fines them for stoppin' away,
   Se wor all in a dother, an' a reglar bother,
   Wi' the wonderful things o' thor modern days.

Thor once wis a time when poor folks in distress,
Could tyek a bit shop, an' get on tee, aw guess,
But noo, the small traders they'll drive te the doors,
For thor's nothin' gans doon but greet factry's and stores,
   Till wor all in a dother, an' a reglar bother,
   Wi' the wonderful things o' thor modern days.

They want a new bridge te cross ower the Tyne,
A reglar High Level byeth costly and fine;
But canny Newcassel's as fly as awd Jocker,
Nowther Gyetsed nor her hes a shot in the locker,
   Se wor all in a dother, an' a reglar bother,
   Wi' the wonderful things o' thor modern days.

When tramways got started, then engines wis tried,
But the horses and cuddies run off or else shied;
Noo, thor runnin' them up and doon hills withoot checks,
Then its off gans the engines and smashes wor necks,
   Till wor all in a dother, an' a reglar bother,
   Wi' the wonderful things o' thor modern days.

In wor plissant bye-roads if ye want a bit talk,
When yor oot wi' yor frind or yor lass for a walk,
No, ye cannot get peace for the road's like a fair
Wi' the bicycle-tricycle demons that's there,
   Se wor all in a dother, an' a reglar bother,
   Wi' the wonderful things o' thor modern days.

They divvent kill folks noo bi one's or bi two's,
But bi hundreds tegether at launches and shows;
And wor man-a-war ships aren't sunk wiv a shot,
But they gan at the fleet an' torpedo the lot,
   Till wor all in a dother, an' a reglar bother,
   Wi' the wonderful things o' thor modern days.

They talk aboot hevin' the electric leet
Doon belaw, and at sea, till there'll be ne mair neet;
But aw'm kind-a-ways jubous 't'ill not come te pass,
Se we better stick oot for wor can'nle and gas,
　　Or else we'll get dothered, an' reg'larly bothered,
　　Wi' the wonderful things o' thor modern days.

Ov the railway and tallygrip often we boast,
But thor noo sendin' all kinds o' parcels bi post,
Such things as bairns' coffins, and brides' weddin'-cakes,
And aw've heerd they send monkeys, and leeches, and
　　snakes,
　　Till wor all in a dother, an' a reglar bother,
　　Wi' the wonderful things o' thor modern days.

Thor wis once nowt but swells went to Parlyment Hoose,
But we noo send wor delegate cheeky and cruse,
For it isn't the claes or the nyem myeks a man,
Se we'll all be't the top o' the tree, if we can,
　　An' we needn't get dothered, nor a little bit bothered,
　　Wi' the wonderful things o' thor modern days.

They wanted a tunnel frev England to France,
Se that folks culd gan dry-shod to lairn hoo te dance;
But they thowt if a hole wis myed under the sea,
We wad all becum French an' eat paddicks te tea,
　　Se wor all in a dother, an' a reglar bother,
　　Wi' the wonderful things o' thor modern days.

But aw'm gettin' case-hardened like Bessemer steel,
For thor's nebody cares what aw think or aw feel,
Se aw'll just jog alang in me awn canny way,
Nivver carin' a farden for what folks may say—
　　Nor aw winnet get dothered, nor a little bit bothered
　　Wi' the wonderful things o' thor modern days

From the North of England Almanac for 1884.

L

TRY AN' MYEK THE WORLD BETTER.

TUNE: "Canny Newcassel."

The world keeps advancin' in modern days,
   Tho' sum dissent like the direckshun;
An' aad fashin'd foaks thinks thor new fangled ways
   Aren't just quite the "pink of perfeckshun."
An' tho' aw admire what's good in the past,
   Aw'm ne ways tied doon te the letter,
For wi' progress we knaw, if it's not ower fast,
   We aye find the world gettin' better.

There once wis a time, tho' thenk hivven! not noo,
   When ne kind ov order existed:
When it might hev been said that, except bi the few,
   The world all improvemint resisted.
But the dawnin' ev knowledge broke ower the sky,
   An' for that we may thenk the type-setter,
For bi beuks and bi readin', thor's nyen can deny
   That the world's been immensely myed better.

Ere the leet o' true wisdom spread ower the land
   Thor wis darkness and vain superstishun,
For 'twas might agyen right, an' the strangor the hand
   The greeter the sway an' posisshun.
But civil-i-zashun com airm'd wi' the pen,
   While freedom broke ivvory fetter;
An' tho' we regret much that's altered an' gyen,
   Yit the world in the main's been myed better.

Thor's sum foaks beleeves that the savage wis bless'd
   When he roam'd throo the prairie at will,
When in just a bit paint or a feather he dress'd,
   An' before he culd eat had te kill.
But aw kind-a-ways think, when a man teuk te claes,
   An' wi' shoes his " poor feet " he did fetter,
That the thowt ov his dress kind o' mended his ways—
   The tailor at leest thinks 'twas better.

Thor's sum thinks that kings, queens, and lords are ne gud,
    But that soshial republics shuld reign;
They wad tyek frae the rich all thor wealth if they culd,
    An' gan in for a new " crowdy-main: "
But cannit republics, like kings, play the fool ?
    Is chaingin' thor nyems onny metter ?
Submisshun te law is society's rool,
    An' till noo, it hes myed the world better.

Thor's others that think we are ower refined
    Wiv elegance, plisshur, an' fashun;
That while, wi' high noshuns wor stuffin' the mind,
    Wor morals wants te gan te the washin'.
Noo this may be true, but it's ony in pairt,
    An' disn't explain the hyel metter.
For religion an' lairnin', an' science an' airt,
    Hev all help'd te myek the world better.

Thor's them that think nations shuld all live at peace,
    An' maistors an' workmen combine;
That the strifes aboot land, aye an' labour, shuld cease:
    Nee doot seck a picture leuks fine;
But the showyest cullors, when put te the test,
    Fade the seunest when dipp'd in the wettor;
An' ne doot as things are, thor ordain'd for the best,
    Then what's best, surely is for the better.

So the sum an' the substance o' what aw've been sayin',
    Is that worth's not a metter o' station,
But each shuld rely on hissel, in the main,
    In helpin' te build up the nation.
Te act upon rules based on honour an' truth,
    Is a law te which each is a debtor,
For it's noble, an' pays in man, woman, or youth,
    Te be helpin' te myek the world better.

From the North of England Almanac for 1885.

WOR AAD FETHER TYNE.

A Soliloquy.

Wor aad Fether Tyne teuk this thowt in his heed,
    One day as he flow'd doon se clivvor:
Ses he tiv hissel, aw mun quicken maw speed,
    For aw'm noo not a common bit river.
Iv coorse aw'm weel knawn as a Royal honor'd stream,
    Wiv ships, docks, and bridges se pritty ;
An' aw knaw aw've drop'd intiv a canny bit seem,
    For aw noo wesh the shores iv a city.

It's all very weel for the Coquet an' Tweed
    Te boast o' thor trout an' thor salmon,
But if they'd the bellies that aw hev te feed
    They'd find a few fishes but gammon.
So seein' aw cum off an up-country race,
    An' flow doon maw valleys se fine,
Aw'll let them all see aw can travel the pace,
    Frev each source te me mouth o' the Tyne.

The Wear an' the Tees may be decent bit streams,
    But they'll ne'er haad a candle te me;
An' tho' they be bouy'd wiv ambishun's fond dreams,
    Thor byeth ower nigh te the sea.
Thor coals an' thor iron are all varry weel—
    They hevent much else, de ye see;
But yor Tyne can supply owthor gunboat or keel,
    An' they've ne place like Newcassel Quay.

For commerce an' trade, wey maw weel fettled stream,
    Wiv it's runners an' feeders te swell her,
An' bonny bit vallies like Derwent and Team,
    And coll'ries like Wallsend and Stella,
An' factories like Airmstrang's an' Stephenson's te,
    And shipyairds like Palmer's at Jarra,
Ne river aw knaw on can cum up te me.
    Aye, aw'm sartin aw hevent a marra.

From the North of England Almanac for 1885.

THE GUD TIMES IN STORE.

TUNE: "The Low-Backed Car."

When things are at the warst, we knaw
　Thor elways sure te mend;
An' though the futor cums but slaw,
　It hes sum gud te send.
Se let's keep up wor hearts, me lads—
　We'll not be eesy doon'd :
An' though the times hev been se bad
　Thor bund te syun cum roond.
　　For we've had the gud times before,
　　An' aw'm shoor thor's gud times in store;
　　So aw'll hope for the best, an' nivvor give in,
　　For aw'm shoor thor's gud times in store.

Ne doot when things wis brisk an' gud,
　Wi' wark an' plenty pay,
We didn't as aw'm shoor we shud,
　Look oot for a rainy day ;
But then what's past we cannot help,
　Spilt-milk isn't worth wor tears,
An' aw'm not gannin' te whinge an' yelp,
　An' upset mesel we fears.
　　For we've had the gud times before, &c.

This yeer's te be a jolly time,
　As them that lives 'll see
Byeth high an' law 'ill all be prime
　At wor Queen's grand Jubilee :
Sic grand like Exhibishuns, ye knaw,
　Wi' bands, an' cullors, an' shows,
An' wondrous things, the foaks te draw
　Bi' thor loyalty or thor nose.
　　For we've had sic like times before, &c.

Noo, Kings an' Queens are varry weel,
　(Aw've ne soshalistic views,)
But cheps that works in a pit or keel
　Hes te mind their P's an' Q's;

An' the fact'ry cheps is just the syem,
 They cannot afford te play;
But if all's rect at wark an' hyem,
 Wey, they like te hev half-a-day.
  For we've had the gud times before, &c.

The wife an' me's been taalkin'd ower,
 The canniest way te de;
Te try an' get the week end ower,
 An' te save a trifle, tee:
Sais aw, wey, de wi' plainor dress,
 Ye need'nt cut such a swell.
Sais she, thor's uthers as bad, aw guess,
 Try that medsin' on yorsel.
  For we've had the gud times before, &c.

So then we've byeth agreed te try
 An' hev a prosp'rous year;
Ne sticky-oot humps she's gan te buy,
 An' aw'm gan te drop the beer.
The young 'uns as they get dune wi' schyule,
 Wor gan te hev put te trade;
For noo wi' lairnin' thor heed's that full,
 That wor fortins 'ill sune be made.
  For we've had the gud times before, &c.

By gum, aw say, what fun thor'll be
 When trade revives at hyem;
Wor plucks 'ill rise an' wor wages tee,
 An' we'll nivvor be poor agyen;
Wor lad shall ride a bicycle then,
 Wor lass the peanna shall play.
The wife an' me 'll croot oot agyen,
 An' we'll get the eight hoors a day.
  For we've had the gud times before, &c.

Then if the Queen shud chance te cum,
 An' the Prince o' Wales an' awl;
We'll byek them singin' hinnies, begum,
 An' ax them te gies a cawl;

An' aw'll dress up se rakish noo,
  The wife 'ill turn oot quite pat,
An' te prove that aw'm byeth loyal an' true
  Aw'll put on me high-top hat.
      For we've had the gud times before, &c.

An' shud the Queen sum honors give—
  Say, a greet lang sword se bright;
Mebbies she'll say te me, by Jove!
  " Rise up, Sor Geordie," Knight!
As labour knights is all the go,
  For me life aw cannot see,
What keeps a title frev me, oh! no,
  At wor Queen's Grand Jubilee.
      For we've had the gud times before, &c.

From the North of England Almanac for 1887.

THE WAY TE BE HAPPY.

TUNE: "Canny Newcassel."

This life's full o' trouble, an' sorrow, an' care,
  An' it tyeks ye te mind hoo ye meet them;
The rich an' the poor, byeth alike he' thor share,
  An' aw doot if there's onny can cheat them;
But still there's a way, if we'll only begin
  When wor yung, life's misfortins te lighten':
It's te guaird weel the tung, an' tyek care o' the tin,
  Then sum comfort woi journey will brighten'.

Fre' the day they leave schule, till thor oot o' thor time,
  Aal yungsters shud keep on advancin';
There's lots to be lairn'd or we get te wor prime,
  An' its better than drinkin' or dancin'.
The lasses shud try hoo te be useful wives,
  An' shud dive inte sewin' an' byekin';
Gud meat an' nice claes help te sweeten wor lives—
  If they divvint aw'm sairly mistyekin'.

A lad an' a lass that hes saved a bit coin,
  An' can manidge te myek a bit livin',
Are just the reet sort that shud marry an' join,
  An' te myek thor twe lives a smaa' hivin';

But this they shud de, an' they nowther shud shirk,
   Keep thor tempers, an' pull weel tegither;
If she minds the hoose an' he sticks tiv his wark,
   They've a fortin' half myed, aw consither.

There's sum hes a trick—an' a silly one te—
   Ov meetin' haalf-way aal thor trubbles;
Sum awful misfortins, or storms they forsee,
   Tho' thor fears often end like "soap bubbles."
Noo life's ower short, wiv its "eight hoors a day,"
   Te work, sleep, an' play, an' the rest on't;
Se when the sun's shinin' let's gether wor hay:
   When it's cloody—wey, just myek the best on't.

Ivery station in life a gud man can adorn,
   Be it sarvint, or foreman, or maistor;
A baronet's title a pit lad hes worn,
   An' a lord hes been knawn for a waistor.
For "honesty is the best policy" still,
   An' respect for the guds ov anuther,
For there's plenty for all, if we work wiv a will,
   Ay, an' sumthin' te spare for a bruther.

Contentment ye'll find's a continewal feast,
   For the envious they always seem snappy,
Gudwill's a gud tenant to hev in yor breest,
   An' it keeps the hoose cheerful an' happy.
Whativvor ye hev elways willinly share,
   For a blessin' rests on the free-giver,
Wi' prudence an' thrift ye need nivver despair,
   An' it helps ye te be a lang liver.

So te sum up the metter, ye lads o' the Tyne,
   An' the Wear, tee, aw warn't aw mun menshun,
For the general gud myek't a rool te combine
   An' avoid a' disputes an' contenshun.
For relidgin an' morals, stick up like a man,
   An' maintain England's grand reputashun,
Nivver folla a cry, nor give up tiv a man,
   What belangs te yor God an' yor Nation.

From the North of England Almanac for 1888.

INDEX.

www.ingramcontent.com/pod-product-compliance
Lightning Source LLC
Chambersburg PA
CBHW020534270326
41927CB00006B/569

9 7 8 3 7 4 4 7 7 5 4 3 4